NATURAL DYES

NATURAL DYES

GWEN FEREDAY

THE BRITISH MUSEUM PRESS

CONTENTS

PART ONE
UNDERSTANDING NATURAL DYES

PART TWO
COLOUR CHARTS & RECIPES

PART ONE
UNDERSTANDING
NATURAL DYES

INTRODUCTION

Nowadays we are bombarded with colours, but so many of them give a rather shallow experience to the discriminating eye. Natural dyes reacquaint us with a high-quality sensory experience that can help to inform and refine our colour sense. I have chosen to work with five of the major historic dyes that have been in use for centuries. I have purposely worked with a limited number of raw materials in order to show something of the extensive range of colours that it is possible to create through mixing, over dyeing and mordanting. Although it is impossible to reproduce all the subtle nuances of some of the colours illustrated in PART TWO of this book, I hope the variety and potential of these permutations are apparent.

Why use natural dyes?

The resonance and richness of natural dyes are impossible to reproduce with synthetic dyes, just as synthetic dyes cannot be replicated by natural dyes. I have in mind certain electric blues and fluorescent colours. Synthetic dyes have a purity and clarity as well as a flatness and harshness depending on how they are used. Although I find these qualities very interesting to work with, I cannot help, however, returning to natural dyes on a regular basis. Whatever wonderful technical advances have been made in the textile trade, the quality and character of natural dyes have not been surpassed.

The danger is that today our expectations are governed by mechanized production. With industrialization, our culture began to lose touch with the raw materials of production, and now it is usual to expect sameness, regularity and standardization. Irregularity is seen as inferior. Although I am not recommending we retreat to a romantic view of the past, there are traditions that we can perpetuate. Quality of colour is definitely one of them.

The process of natural dyeing

The preparation and application of natural dyes is a complex process, involving a series of treatments that varies according to the chosen fibre and desired end-colour. When something is dyed, tiny molecules of soluble coloured matter stick to the fibres of the material being dyed. This sticking process is strengthened by mordants (metallic salts) that increase the dyestuff's ability to bond with the fibre and help improve its fastness. The techniques involved in this process are fascinating and varied and have been developed over many centuries.

The development of natural dyes

While it is not known exactly when natural dyes were invented, they have been in use for thousands of years in many regions of the world. From the time people started dyeing, they would have collected their own ingredients and experimented with what was available. Knowledge would have been passed on orally and kept within the family, tribe or clan. Dyes, their recipes and their usage were regionally distinctive. While some cultures still maintain their distinctive regional identity, the general trend has been towards diffusion. Regular trading routes played their part in this, making available new exotic dyes and materials, which enabled the establishment of larger-scale, less localized production.

Revival and continuity

The invention and growing use of synthetic dyes in the nineteenth century contributed to a loss of knowledge that had been gathered over centuries. In the early twentieth century, Ethel Mairet (1872–1952) and Elizabeth Peacock (1880–1969), pioneers in the rediscovery of the craft tradition of woven textiles in Britain, undertook valuable research into dyeing pratices.

Ella McLeod (1908–2000), who was responsible for the development of the textile department at the West Surrey College of Art and Design in Farnham (now the Surrey Institute of Art and Design, University College or SIAD), had direct links with these pioneers. Ella's connections with this on-going craft movement fed into her work in education and her collaborations with colleagues.

One of her colleagues, Margaret Bide, was my tutor when I studied weaving and dyeing at Farnham in the early 1970s. She gave me access to recipes and information which she, in turn, had gathered. All this proved invaluable to this project since it has given me the confidence and freedom to experiment and develop my colours, particularly in the dyeing of cellulose fibres, and very particularly in the development of the colour Turkey red.

This book represents an introduction to colour mixing and verifies the validity of continuing to work with time-consuming natural dyestuffs.

HOW TO USE THIS BOOK

The book has been divided into two parts: PART ONE introduces you to the various processes involved in natural dyeing and gives you an overall view of the sources of natural colour; PART TWO is devoted to colour charts, showing a wide spectrum of colours, accompanied by individual recipes. The colours in the charts use only the five historic dyes of madder, indigo, cutch, cochineal and weld, combined with a range of mordants (fixatives) and treatments. The colour charts are broadly based on a 'twelve-hue colour wheel' and there are over five hundred shades from which to choose. You may have an idea of a particular colour that you would like to produce, or you can use the colour swatches in PART TWO for inspiration.

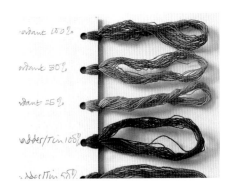

Keeping accurate records of what you have done and how you have done it is vital.

Recipes

PART ONE contains recipes that demonstrate the basic techniques involved in dyeing both animal fibres, such as wool and silk, and vegetable fibres, such as cotton and linen. These are written out in full and form the basis of the abbreviated, but more particular, recipes in PART TWO.

PART TWO is sub-divided into recipes for animal and vegetable fibres. The recipes are numbered – each number relates to a colour shade on the opposite page. The abbreviated recipes are written in the order of procedure, and give the quantities of ingredients needed. They cross-refer to the recipes in PART ONE, and any deviations from the basic recipes are written in *italics*.

KEY TO ABBREVIATIONS:
g = gram/s
ml = millilitre/s
sec = second/s
min = minute/s
hr = hour/s
% = percentage (of dry weight of material)
°C = degrees Centigrade

Quantities

This book uses the metric system for its precision and suitability to small quantities. A conversion chart on p.104 gives imperial and US measures. Unless otherwise stated, the recipes are based on using 100g of dry weight yarn. The quantities for most of the other ingredients in the recipes are expressed as a percentage of the dry weight of material. This is simple when you are using 100g of yarn; for example 20% madder dye is 20g, 30% is 30g, 40% is 40g, and so on. Millilitres are equivalent to grams, therefore 4% acetic acid is equal to 4ml of acetic acid. For less obvious weights of yarn, this is the formula: Percentage equals number divided by 100, multiplied by the weight of the material divided by 1, for example,

$$5\% \text{ of } 50g = \frac{5}{100} \times \frac{50}{1} = 2.5g$$

Colour charts in PART TWO

All these colours have been achieved using madder, cochineal, weld, indigo and cutch, combined with a range of mordants and other treatments, such as tannic acid treatment or Turkey red oil treatment.

Each colour has been wound onto a card, and each card has three shades of the same colour: a dark, a medium and a pale, arranged from left to right. Sometimes the tonal difference between the colours is quite marked and at other times it is less apparent. More dyestuff may result in a denser shade or a warmer or cooler effect. These differences are occasionally very subtle but I have chosen to keep them as part of the record.

The materials

Yarn skeins or hanks (loosely coiled bundles of yarn) have been used in all the recipes in this book. For the recipes in PART TWO, I have used a worsted merino wool as the animal fibre because it takes dye well. For the vegetable fibres, I have chosen a mercerized cotton because it absorbs the dye more readily than other vegetable fibres. The recipes can be adapted for use on other materials, such as unspun fibres and cloth (*see* pp.16–17).

It should be noted that individual materials absorb colour differently; it is not just the difference between how animal and veg-etable fibres react to dyes. If you want to match a colour, it is crucial to carry out tests using samples of the required fibre.

Keeping records

Maintaining clear and accurate notes on what you have done and how you have done it is very important for good professional practice. It enables you to repeat a colour and also helps you to trouble-shoot if some-thing goes wrong or happens unexpectedly.
• Always keep a sample of the colour.
• Record quantities of yarn, water, fixatives and dyestuff accurately.
• Record the pH of the water you use, as this can affect the colours obtained.
• Record the length of time taken to reach a temperature, what the temperature was and precisely how long the temperature was maintained.
• Record how long the material remained in the dye liquor.
• Record the order of the procedure: for example, was the mordant used before dyeing, or with the dye, or added as an after mordant.
• Label the finished material.

Testing for light-fastness

All colours deteriorate in time, and natural dyes are no exception. Some colours can become darker or duller when repeatedly exposed to light, while others simply become paler. If you have worked hard to achieve a particular shade, it is important to know how it is likely to change with time, especially if you are designing with more than one colour in mind. Mixing a colour by over dyeing one dye with another can also pose potential problems if one colour

outlasts the other. This is why so many medieval tapestries have blue forests and grass, the yellows having faded in advance of the blues. When testing your colours at home for light-fastness:
• Mount them in between two pieces of card, leaving half the sample exposed.
• Leave your samples for one month in a window that does not get direct sunlight.
• Check them every seven days and remove a portion of each sample for your records. This will indicate clearly how the colours change week by week, as well as how quickly this happens.
• You may choose to leave your samples exposed to the light for a longer period of time, in which case if you intend to remove a portion of the sample each week you obviously need to allow sufficient material for this from the outset.
• The time of year is significant too, and this should remain as constant as possible.

Testing for wash-fastness

Everyone has experienced the frustration of one dye bleeding onto another in a mixed wash. To establish how fast your colours are to washing:
• Test your yarn by plying (twisting) the dyed yarn with a length of undyed yarn. Wash the samples in a warm soap solution.
• Keep another unwashed sample aside for comparison.
• If the sample being tested colours the undyed yarn, it can be assumed that it may colour other materials that it is placed next to.
• Some colour may wash out but not affect the undyed yarn, though the dyed yarn may look paler than before.
• To see if there is a marked difference you can wind the samples onto card for easy comparison.

Health and safety

• Treat all your materials as a potential hazard unless you know otherwise.
• Keep mordanting and dyeing away from food and food preparation areas.
• Never eat, drink or smoke while working.
• Store materials in a cool, dry place, clearly labelled and in well-sealed containers.
• Keep materials out of direct light and away from pets and children.
• Always work in a well-ventilated environment.
• Wear protective clothing, gloves, overalls and a mask to protect against dust and fumes.
• Keep lids on mordant and dye baths to reduce fumes.
• Add acids to water, *never* add water to acids, to reduce fumes, and splashing.
• Follow handling instructions on mordants, mordant assistants and dyestuffs.
• Mordants are particularly hazardous (*see* pp.24–5).
• It is often better to simmer your material than to boil it, since some mordants, such as chrome (potassium di/bichromate), give off toxic fumes when boiled.
• Always dispose of spent mordant liquor and dye material carefully, down the lavatory rather than the sink.
• It is advisable to contact your local public analyst or your sewage company for advice, if you are working on a large scale.

COLOUR

Working with colour is very personal. Colour has the capacity to evoke all sorts of emotions. While few of us have the opportunity to really study its potential as a visual language, the more you work with colour the more sensitive you will become to it. Colours never stand still, they are constantly changing as the light changes. We only have to observe our surroundings during a sunset. Colours can become quite luminous in a golden light whereas a sharp early morning light will give a totally different experience. This phenomenon has held the imagination of artists for centuries and explains why so many of them return again and again to the same subject in an attempt to capture its essence.

The science of colour

The human eye is said to perceive in the region of ten million colours or shades. Colour does not exist without light. Our brain interprets the light received through our eyes as colour. We are made aware of colour and light by means of a series of cones and rods that are situated in the retina, the lining at the back of the eyeball. The rods deal with tone, that is light to dark or absence of colour, like a black and white photograph. The cones deal with colour; there are three sets of cones: one set of cones is sensitive to red, one to green and the third to violet. There are thought to be in the region of seven million cones and one hundred and twenty million rods in each eye, and one million nerve fibres connecting the retina to the optic nerve which, in turn, connects to the brain.

Colour is revealed by light reflecting back off surfaces after partial absorption. Total absorption reveals black or lack of light, while no absorption reveals white or total light. Though light is white, when it is broken up by passing through a prism or water, the light rays separate into wave-bands of different lengths and we see what Isaac Newton (1642–1727) recorded seeing in the mid seventeenth century, a rainbow of colours: red, orange, yellow, green, blue, indigo and violet.

The theory of colour

Colour can appear to change depending on which colour surrounds it. For instance, if a neutral grey is placed next to a red it will give the impression of being a greenish grey, whereas if the same grey is next to a blue, it will take on an orange tinge. This was called a simultaneous contrast by the French dye chemist Michel Eugène Chevreul (1786–1889), director of the dye works at the Gobelin tapestry factory in Paris. He also worked out a colour scale that was determined by three variables: hue, saturation and lightness. Hue refers to the colour itself; saturation to the intensity of a colour; and lightness refers to the lightness or darkness of a colour, its tone.

The twelve-hue colour wheel

The colours in PART TWO are loosely based on the 'twelve-hue colour wheel' as devised by Isaac Newton and developed by Johannes Itten (1888–1967), a dominant figure in the Bauhaus design school from 1919 to 1923.

The wheel starts with the three primary colours of red, yellow and blue. There are two types of colour: those associated with light, called additive colours, and those associated with pigment, known as subtractive colours. For the purpose of this book we only look at colours associated with pigment since they relate to dyes.

The three subtractive primary colours are red, yellow and blue, or strictly speaking magenta (blueish red), yellow and cyan (greenish blue), as used in the printing trade. All the colours of the spectrum can be produced by mixing the primary subtractive colours. This is known as subtractive mixing. Secondary colours are achieved when two primary colours are combined to make orange, violet and green. Tertiary colours are created by mixing a primary with a secondary to make yellow-orange, orange-red, red-violet, violet-blue, blue-green and green-yellow.

At a glance, the wheel can be used to find complementary colours. Each colour has a complementary secondary colour. Red is the complementary of green, a mixture of yellow and blue; yellow is the complementary of violet, a mixture of red and blue; and blue is the complementary of orange, a mixture of yellow and red.

While this system underpins the colour charts in PART TWO, it is important to point out that I have not allowed it to limit my exploration of colour. While other people's theories have contributed to my understanding and appreciation, my ultimate choice of colour is driven by personal aesthetic judgement.

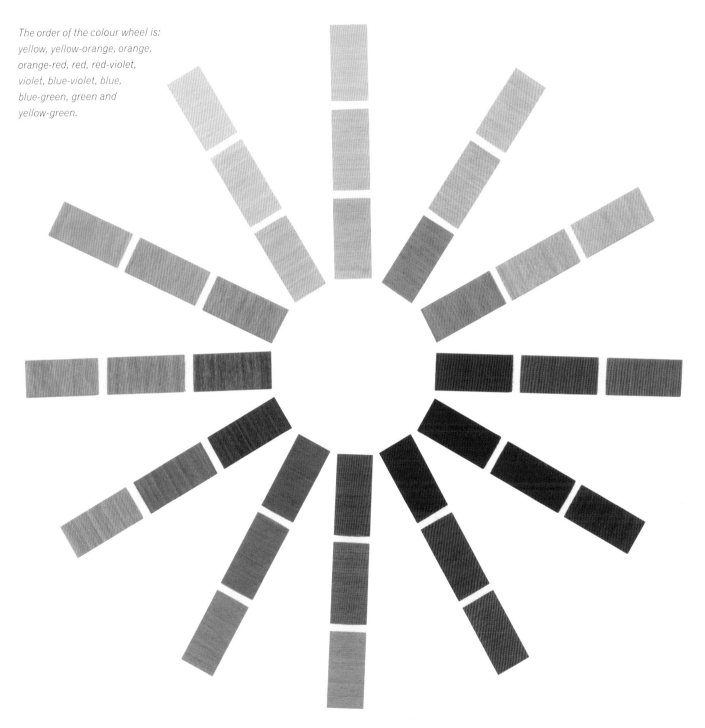

The order of the colour wheel is: yellow, yellow-orange, orange, orange-red, red, red-violet, violet, blue-violet, blue, blue-green, green and yellow-green.

FACILITIES AND EQUIPMENT

For those who are about to commence dyeing, it is important to find a dedicated space to work in, which is not compromised or confused with any other activity. Dyeing should not be undertaken in your kitchen; pots and utensils for dyeing and those for food preparation must be kept entirely separate. The space should be well ventilated, with access to hot and cold water, a heat source (I find it easier to control the temperature with gas rather than electricity), shelves for storage, easy access to a washing line or dryer and ideally a door with a lock, so that any inquisitive children only enter under supervision. While much of the equipment you need can be bought in a kitchen shop, there is a list of specialist suppliers on p.100.

Dye pots
Stainless steel containers for mordanting and dyeing are best because they are easy to clean and are inert, that is they won't affect the colour you are trying to achieve.

Colanders and strainers
A stainless steel colander or strainer is useful for separating the dye liquor from the dyestuff and is helpful for preventing blocked drains. I always keep a strainer device in my sink as a precaution against blocking.

Buckets
Plastic or stainless steel buckets are useful for washing and filling the dye baths and emptying them.

Stirring rods and tongs
I use plastic or stainless steel stirring rods. Plastic or stainless steel tongs can be useful but are not essential; I tend to use my stirring rods for lifting yarns instead.

Measuring instruments
Plastic, glass or stainless steel measuring jugs or beakers vary in size, but those with a litre and a half litre capacity are particularly useful. Plastic syringes are good for measuring smaller quantities of liquid. Stainless steel spoons are useful for measuring out the mordants and dyes.

Metric scales
Laboratory balance scales are crucial for measuring small quantities accurately.

Thermometer
A kitchen or laboratory thermometer is essential for checking the temperature of the dye bath.

Clock or watch
A clock or watch is essential for accurate timing of mordanting and dyeing.

Protective clothing
A protective cotton overall, rubber gloves and a face mask are vital. I use cotton-lined PVC gloves because they are stronger than ordinary rubber gloves and more resistant to heat, but many people use thin disposable gloves. Use heat-proof oven gloves for lifting hot lids and pans. Use a protective face mask when measuring out mordants and any fine powders or when poisonous materials are being simmered or boiled.

Sealed jars
Glass jars with good seals and clear labels for dyes and mordants are essential as some of the ingredients are poisonous. They must be stored safely on shelves which are out of direct sunlight, in a cool place and beyond the reach of children and pets.

Grinder
Some dye stuffs may need grinding down to assist dyeing. For this a pestle and mortar can be used but I prefer to use a coffee grinder, especially for cochineal.

Steamer
For the oil treatment traditionally used to produce the colour Turkey red, you need a steamer. If you do not have access to an industrial one, it is possible to steam the yarn using a double-saucepan system. I rigged up a wire basket on top of my mordant bath and fitted a lid on top of that.

A selection of smaller items
Other useful items include: scissors; matches if you use gas; pH papers for testing water; a pencil and notebook for keeping records; labels; paper bags; polythene bags; a drying rack or line; paper and cloth towels; cleaning materials; scourers and ordinary cloths; soap; card, a Stanley knife and a hole puncher for cutting cards ready for mounting yarn for home light-fast testing and general recording purposes; strong undyed cotton thread for tying up skeins and bundles of harvested dyestuff for drying purposes; and skein-winding equipment (*see* p.18).

1 *Metric scales* 2 *Strainer* 3 *Stirring rod* 4 *Rubber gloves* 5 *Bucket*
6 *Colander* 7 *Stainless steel dye bath* 8 *Measuring beakers* 9 *PH papers*
10 *Scourer* 11 *Measuring jugs* 12 *Stainless steel spoons* 13 *Thermometer*
14 *Coffee grinder* 15 *Stirring rod* 16 *Face mask*

CHOOSING MATERIALS

All fibres have their own particular characteristics, and choosing which fibre to work with depends entirely on the end result you have in mind. I only refer to materials that occur in nature as these were the fibres available to the dyer before the use of synthetic dyes. These fall into two categories: animal fibres and vegetable fibres, and both need to be treated differently. There are, however, certain fibres that are man-made but derived from natural sources, for example rayon is made from cellulose and can be dyed using the vegetable recipes. Since all fibres absorb colour differently, it is advisable to run a few tests before making your final choice. Remember to record every stage so that you can analyse the results.

FROM TOP TO BOTTOM *The animal fibres represented here include several varieties of wools such as Merino and Cheviot wool. The bottom two animal fibres are spun cultivated silk and wild tussah silk.*

Durability

It is important to test your material for durability. Natural dyeing is a lengthy process and your material has to be strong enough to withstand rigorous treatments. Natural dyes take at least twice as long as synthetic dyes to get a result, but the colours you produce will make the effort worthwhile.

Dyeing different types of fibre

This book deals with dyeing yarn, but you may wish to dye cloth or unspun fibres instead. There are drawbacks when working with unspun fibres and cloth, which need to be overcome:

• As unspun fibres tend to swell up in water, they will need to be kept in an open meshed bag with extra water. Because the fibres are concentrated together, this could result in the uneven absorption of colour, the centre of the mass being paler than the outer fibres.
• Cloth often sticks to itself and traps air bubbles in between its layers, resulting in a tendency to float to the surface and therefore not to take the mordant and dye evenly.

The following steps should reduce the likelihood of uneven dyeing for both unspun fibres and cloth:

1 Use a larger dye bath and regularly move and spread out the material gently.
2 Do not overfill the dye bath with material, ensuring easy movement during scouring, mordanting and dyeing.
3 Thorough rinsing at every stage is also important for removing loosely attached mordant and dye.

Animal fibres

Animal fibres are made of protein and are obtained from animals, such as wool from sheep, as well as insects, as in the case of silk. Alpaca, vicuna, llama, angora, camel, mohair and cashmere are some of the more exotic animal fibres that are available. They all have their own particular characteristics and qualities and it takes time to become familiar with each of them.

Wool

Wool describes the hairy covering of several species of quadrupeds – sheep and goats being the most common. Once the fleece is removed from the animal, the fibres are spun into threads. Wool takes dye very well and is a generous and versatile material. Of all the textile fibres, wool tends to be the most variable in type and quality and can be made into fabrics of diverse appearance and application. Wool can be used to make light-weight summer clothes, heavy winter garments, upholstery fabrics and carpeting. Some nomadic tribes still use it to make their felt tents, which can withstand extreme heat and cold as well as keep out the wind and rain.

Wool comes in many forms: some wools are lustrous and smooth while others

The vegetable fibres shown here include half-bleached Swedish linen; bleached Swedish linen; unbleached Irish linen; unbleached Irish linen; mercerized cotton; cotton and cotton slub.

are soft and fluffy. Under magnification a wool fibre has the appearance of overlapping roof-tiles; these platelets vary in size according to the breed of the animal and its living conditions. The fibre with the longer platelets tends to be more lustrous. It is these platelets that move and allow the fibre to shrink under certain conditions, giving wool its diversity and elasticity.

Felting

The composition of wool makes it liable to felt easily and if sufficient care is not taken, unwanted felting or sticking together of the yarn could contribute to uneven dye results. The following steps will lessen the likelihood of this problem occurring:

1 Avoid over soaping when scouring.
2 Do not rush the cleaning process.
3 Avoid running water directly onto woollen yarn.
4 Make sure the yarn is fully wetted out (saturated with water) before mordanting or dyeing begins.
5 Do not subject wool to vigorous movement during the dyeing process.
6 Never subject wool to sudden changes of temperature or boiling; gentle simmering is generally sufficient.

Silk

Silk is an animal fibre made from the cocoons of silkworms. The long fibres of the cocoons are unwound and spun into threads. It can be cultivated or wild. Silk absorbs colour well, but needs to be treated with care. It has less elasticity than wool and can lose its lustre if boiled too rigorously. Silk is also vulnerable to sunlight and will rot if subjected to too much of it.

Alkalis and acids

Animal fibres are adversely affected by alkalis, such as washing soda, household ammonia, lime or chalk, but they are not affected by acids, such as acetic acid or vinegar, citric acid or lemon juice. This is the reverse of vegetable fibres and explains why these two types of material require different treatments before dyeing can begin.

Vegetable fibres

Vegetable fibres are made up of cellulose, which consists largely of glucose or sugar. The main plant fibres that are used in the textile industry are cotton, linen, jute, hemp and ramie. All have their particular characteristics. Vegetable fibres take longer than animal fibres to prepare and dye because of the cellular structure of the fibre.

Cotton

Cotton is a versatile material that is used to make a wide range of articles from fine cotton handkerchieves to hard-wearing hammocks. It is a seed fibre, obtained from the white fluffy fibres that protect the seeds of the cotton plant. Under magnification the cotton fibres appear to consist of multiple hair-like strands, which wrap round each other in a spiral formation. This is what gives cotton a little more elasticity than linen, which consists of long straight strands of fibre made from stalks of the flax plant. The fibres tend to run parallel to each other. It is the fibres' length that gives linen its lustre and is the reason why it is so susceptible to creasing.

In the colour charts in PART TWO I have used mercerized cotton, which is a cotton treated under tension with caustic soda. This has the effect of strengthening the fibres, improving their dyeability and making the fibres lustrous, giving the cotton a silk-like quality.

Colour matching

Wool is easier to match than most dyes since it tends to keep a similar depth of shade between its damp and dry stage.

When silk is in the dye bath, it looks much darker than it will be once it has been rinsed and dried.

After dyeing and rinsing vegetable fibres, the colour will dry at least fifty per cent paler than it appears when damp. Lastly, when choosing your yarn, you will need to consider its natural colour. A naturally brown or buff-coloured yarn can only be used for darker shades, while a white fibre is needed for pale, pure shades.

PREPARING MATERIALS

To ensure that dye colour is absorbed evenly, materials need to be properly prepared. All the care taken in these early stages will be rewarded by a satisfying end result. Whether you choose unspun fibres, cloth or yarns, all materials must be thoroughly cleaned. The process by which materials are completely removed of all dirt, waxes, oils and grease is called 'scouring'. It is a vital procedure as any grease or dirt will act as a resist against the mordant and dye and give you an uneven result. If you are using yarn, you will need to wind it into a skein before scouring can commence. A correctly wound and tied skein makes yarn manageable and prevents tangling during the dyeing process.

Quantities for dyeing

Before you start the dyeing process, you need to know the dry weight of the yarn since this dictates the amount of mordant and dyestuff you need to achieve the colour you are aiming for. Skeins are usually 50g or 100g in weight.

Winding a skein

If you are new to tying skeins, start by winding with a relatively thick, naturally white wool yarn. If you work with very fine fibres, it can take a long time to prepare and a fine skein is much more likely to become tangled during the dyeing process.

There are a number of ways to help you create even skeins, once you have chosen your desired weight of yarn.

1 Spinners will be familiar with the niddy-noddy, which is an ingenious device. It consists of a centre bar, with two cross pieces at either end, set at right angles to each other. By attaching the end of the yarn to one of the end sticks and winding in a figure of eight motion a skein of any size can be made.

2 Weavers will be familiar with warping pegs, which are set into a block of wood which is clamped to a table. The yarn is wound around the pegs, which can be adjusted to any length. As you wind the skein, ensure that each rotation has the same tension and is evenly spaced. Keep the yarn attached to the warping pegs, ready for tying.

3 An alternative method requires no financial outlay: use the posts of two wooden dining-chairs, placed back to back. Attach the end of the yarn to one of the chairposts, and then wind the yarn around

LEFT *Undyed yarn can be bought in a variety of forms from cones to ready-made skeins.*

the chairposts until the skein is complete. Keep the skein on the posts until you have tied the skein with new cotton yarn.

A manufacturer's skein

If the yarn comes from the manufacturers as a skein, you will need to undo any existing ties as these are often too tight or too loose, and replace them with new tying-up cotton to prevent tangling. A rice is a particularly useful, but not an essential, holding device on which to place a manufacturer's skein ready for tying.

Tying a skein

Tie the skein using a strong undyed cotton yarn which is different from the yarn you are dyeing. You need to be able to identify your ties since they help you to restore order to the skein at every stage of the dyeing process. You should use cotton for wool skeins too.

Remember not to make the skein ties too tight as this will prevent the mordant and dye from penetrating the skein evenly and cause a tie-dye effect.

Tying the ends of the skein

1 Stretch out your skein.
2 Check the threads are running parallel to each other.
3 Find the ends of the skein and re-tie them with an overhand knot. To tie an overhand knot hold the two ends together, wrap the ends around on themselves to form a loop, then pass the two ends through the loop and pull to tighten.
4 Cut a length of tying-up cotton, and place it around the width of the skein.
5 Join the ends of the skein with the two ends of the tying-up cotton in an overhand knot. (*See* diagram 1.) This clearly identifies the two ends of the skein for later use.

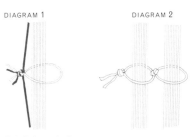

Additional ties

1 Cut a length of tying-up cotton and place it around the width of the skein. Remember that when yarn is wet, it expands, so the ties need to allow for this and yet not be so loose that they move freely round the skein and form a clump.
2 Sub-divide the skein into sections and wrap a length of cotton round the first section and secure with an overhand knot.
3 Take the ends of the tying-up cotton, and place one on each side of the next section and secure with another knot. (*See* diagram 2.) Often you only need to divide your skein in half, but if the skein is larger than 50g, or the yarn is particularly fine, you may need to split the yarn into further sections.
4 Check that you have allowed sufficient movement of the threads within each split section, otherwise they will stick together.
5 Move round the skein and repeat this at three equally spaced intervals. You may wish to add more ties depending on the fineness of the yarn and the size of the skein. The ties should be split in different places across the skein each time to stop the ties from clumping.
6 Finally tie one long cotton tie round the width of the skein, so the skein can be lifted easily in and out of the mordant or dye bath. (*See* diagram 3.)

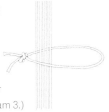

ABOVE *Two skeins of yarn are stretched on a rice. The cone of strong, undyed cotton yarn is suitably different from the yarns to use as a tie that will stand out.*

BELOW *The knot used for tying a skein is the overhand knot.*

SCOURING ANIMAL FIBRES

It is important to make sure that scouring is not rushed and that the yarn is fully wetted out (saturated with water) before mordanting or dyeing begins. Different animal fibres require different treatments. In particular, the composition of wool makes it liable to felt easily and if sufficient care is not taken, unwanted felting or sticking together of the yarn could contribute to uneven dye results.

Scouring wool (*Based on a SIAD recipe*)
1 Soak the securely tied skeins (*see* p.19) in a bucket of hand-hot water for approximately 10 minutes. Allow 3–4 litres of water per 100g of yarn. This will loosen any grease or dirt that is in the yarn.
2 Remove and gently hand-wring the skein.
3 Prepare a bucket of fresh hand-hot water to which you have added sufficient soap flakes to create a lather.
4 Add the yarn and steep it in the soapy water for approximately 10 minutes.
5 Remove and gently hand-wring the skein.

6 Repeat with fresh soapy water, reducing the amount of soap each time until all the grease has been removed. When the washing water remains soapy, the grease has been removed.
7 Remove and hand-wring the skein.
8 Rinse in hand-hot water and repeat until the water is completely clear, taking care not to run hot tap water directly onto the yarn as this can cause felting.

Scouring silk (*Based on a SIAD recipe*)
Silk requires boiling in soap solution in order to clean it thoroughly and to remove the gum that has been left by the silkworm. Any residues of gum will react as a resist to both mordant and dye.

1 Fill a stainless steel bowl with enough hot water to comfortably cover the material being scoured. Allow 3–4 litres of water per 100g of dry weight of yarn.
2 Add a handful of soap flakes.
3 Place the skeins in the prepared bath and bring them to the boil. Different silks require different boiling times:
White (cultivated) silk – 10 minutes.
Tussah (wild) silk – 20 minutes.
It is important not to boil silk too vigorously or for too long as this seems to have a harshening effect on the fibre.
4 Retain the boiling-off liquid in which to re-immerse the skeins after dyeing. This helps to return the lustre to the yarn.
5 Rinse until water is clear.
6 Spin dry and straighten skein, and use as soon as possible.

Scouring wool
STEP 4 *Place the skein in hot, soapy water*

STEP 6 *Soak the skein in soapy water*

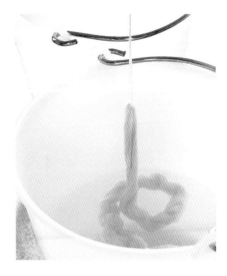

STEP 8 *Rinse the wool skein in clear water*

SCOURING VEGETABLE FIBRES

Vegetable fibres have a natural wax which needs to be thoroughly removed since it could act as a resist and prevent the mordant or dye from attaching to the fibres. To thoroughly clean vegetable fibres it is necessary to boil the fibres in a solution of washing soda (sodium carbonate). Unlike wool, vegetable fibres can be boiled without fear of felting due to their different structure and material composition.

Scouring cotton and linen

(Based on a SIAD recipe)

CHEMICAL INGREDIENTS

Washing soda

Acetic acid

1 Clean the scales straight after you have measured the washing soda to prevent the washing soda from attacking the surface.
2 Dissolve 5g washing soda in 1 litre of hand-hot water. Allow 3–4 litres of water to each 100g of yarn.
3 Place the securely tied skeins into the boiling-off solution and bring to the boil.

Different yarns require different boiling times:
Mercerized cotton – 20 minutes.
Non-mercerized cotton – 30 minutes.
Unbleached linen – 30 minutes.
Bleached linen – 15 minutes.
4 After boiling, allow the solution to cool and remove the skein carefully.
5 Wring out the surplus liquid before rinsing the skeins in hot water.
6 Rinse in fresh hot water until the water appears clear.
7 For the final rinse add 10ml of acetic acid

per litre of water. Vinegar contains 5% acetic acid. If you use vinegar instead you need to use 60ml of vinegar per litre.
8 Hand-wring, shake out and straighten the skeins to ensure the yarn has not become tangled; it is now ready for the next stage.

Water

Water will vary in its acidity or alkalinity depending on its origins, and natural dye colours can alter according to the quality of the water used. Neutral water is generally seen to be the best water to dye with, and rain water used to be collected for this purpose. Today, however, with acid rain problems rain water may not be neutral. The water I used to achieve the colours in PART TWO had a pH of 7.

Testing the water pH

To test for the acidity or alkalinity of your water you need to purchase a book of pH papers. PH papers are a golden yellow colour and have a colour guide on their outer cover with numbers from 1–11. PH 7 is neutral, and any number below 7 refers to the acidity of a substance and anything above 7 refers to the alkalinity of substance. Variations on the pH from 5.5–8.5 will not drastically affect the colour being dyed. It only becomes a problem if you are trying to match a particular colour and the water is preventing you from obtaining it.

To alter the water pH

To make water more alkaline, add a little washing soda (sodium carbonate), household ammonia or chalk. To make water more acidic, add a little acetic acid or clear vinegar. It is possible to use these to modify a colour after it has been dyed, but remember to rinse the yarn in neutral water afterwards.

Scouring cotton
STEP 2 *Add washing soda to boiling off bath*

STEP 3 *Add the skein and bring to the boil*

MORDANTS

Mordanting, a critical step in the dyeing process, is a means of treating the fibre to ensure that the colour fixes onto it. It usually increases the fastness of the colour and can extend the range of hues that can be obtained from the dyestuff. The most common mordants are metallic salts such as alum, chrome, iron, tin and copper, and are applied either before, during or after dyeing, depending on the recipe. Sometimes mordants are combined with substances known as 'assistants', such as oxalic acid: these allow for a more efficient take up of the mordant. Some plants also contain mordanting ingredients, for example there are residues of oxalic acid in rhubarb leaves, but it is difficult to know the exact amount of mordant present.

Mordant action

Since most natural dyes do not have a natural affinity with textile fibres, they need a mordant to make the fibres receptive to the dye. When a material is dyed, tiny molecules of soluble coloured matter stick to the fibres being dyed. This process is strengthened by mordants – chemicals that increase the dyes' ability to stick to the fibre and help improve its fastness.

Mordant effects

Each mordant has its own characteristics and affects the ultimate colour in different ways. For example, tin is often used to brighten colours, while iron is used to sadden colours. Substantive dyes, such as cutch and walnut husks, do not need a mordant to fix the dye, but mordants may be added to improve light-fastness or as a colour modifier.

Mordant assistants

Assistants combine with the mordant and help the dye to attach itself to the fibre in a more permanent state, as well as allowing for less mordant to be used.

Applying the mordant

Although animal and vegetable fibres require different mordant treatments, these guidelines relate to both fibres:

1 The exact amount of water is not crucial, but there must be sufficient water to allow the fibres to move freely and ensure that they remain below the surface of the mordant solution at all times.

2 All fibres need to be fully wetted out (saturated with water) before mordanting.

3 It is important not to rush the process as this could adversely affect the way the dye takes and could cause an uneven and unstable dye result.

4 Thorough rinsing away of surplus unattached mordant is crucial so the dye can properly attach itself to the fibre.

Pre-mordanting

Most fibres are pre-mordanted, which means that the yarn is mordanted first and then dyed in a separate dye bath. You can mordant skeins in advance of dyeing and store them for later use. However, it is important to label them and store them separately to avoid contamination or confusion; it is not always easy to distinguish one mordanted skein from another. If mordanted skeins are stored, care must be taken to ensure that they are adequately wetted out before dyeing can commence.

One-bath method

Not all fibres are mordanted before dyeing. For some it is more appropriate to include the mordant in the same bath as the dye. This is known as the 'one-bath method'.

After mordanting

If the mordant is added after dyeing it is known as an 'after mordant'. Strictly speaking an after mordant is prepared in a separate dye bath and the dyed material is added to the mordant bath straight away, without being rinsed. However, sometimes a mordant is added to the dye bath towards the end of the dyeing process.

Mordanting animal fibres

Heat encourages mordant action but with wool it needs to be applied cautiously to prevent unwanted felting or shrinkage (see p.17). Silk also needs to be handled with care. In order to preserve the silk's lustre, it is advisable to use lower heating temperatures than those used for wool.

Mordanting vegetable fibres

Mordanting vegetable fibres is more involved than mordanting animal fibres, but the results are so exciting, it is well worth spending the extra time. After scouring, the yarn will normally need to be treated with tannic acid before it is ready for mordanting. This ensures the most efficient take up of dye. Vegetable fibres take longer to wet out too. Linen may need to be simmered for longer than cotton because it is more resistant to dye take up.

Safety guidelines

- If you are not sure whether a substance is toxic or not, assume it is; this will ensure professional practice at all times.
- Get into the habit of wearing a face mask when measuring out fine powders and toxic substances.
- An overall and rubber gloves will protect you from splashing.
- Never measure out mordants near food or drink.
- Keep all mordants and mordant assistants in clearly labelled containers.
- Keep mordants and assistants out of reach of children and pets.
- Keep all mordants and mordant assistants out of direct sunlight, preferably locked away in a cool place.
- If mordant powders or crystals make skin contact, wash off thoroughly with water and remove any contaminated clothing.
- Acids, such as formic acid and acetic acid, can cause severe burns if they come into contact with skin and eyes.
- If acid does touch the skin, bathe the affected area thoroughly in cold water for at least ten minutes and obtain medical attention.
- If acids or mordants are inhaled, withdraw from exposure, rest and keep warm. In severe cases, obtain medical attention as soon as possible.
- If acids or mordants are ingested, wash mouth out with water and drink plenty of water. You should obtain medical attention.
- *Never* add water to acids, always add acids to water.
- Never rush at any stage as this is when mistakes occur and accidents happen.

Mordants and assistants

The recipes in this book use a variety of mordants and mordant assistants that can be purchased from reputable suppliers (*see* p.100). Such mordants have been in use for centuries. An Indus Valley excavation unearthed cloth that had been dyed with the aid of a mordant dating back to 2,000 BC, and the Roman scholar Pliny the Elder referred to the use of mordants in Egypt in the first century AD. The sophistication of the methods used implies that mordants were well established by then.

Alum (potassium aluminium sulphate or potash alum)
Alum comes in the form of white crystals or powder. Though non-toxic, it can be an irritant if inhaled. It is the oldest known mordant, and was used in India as far back as 2,000 BC. Alum can be used on all fibres and keeps colours pure. It is mostly used as a pre-mordant. The mordanted yarn is best used in its damp state after mordanting, as wetting out is difficult once alummed yarn has been allowed to dry. Alum-mordanted yarn is sometimes wrapped in a damp cloth and left to mature for a few days to improve dye results. An excess of alum on wool can make the yarn permanently sticky to handle. Once this happens, the stickiness cannot be removed by washing or rinsing.

Chrome (potassium bichromate/dichromate)
Chrome's orange crystals turn a sage green after oxidation. It is poisonous and can cause an allergic reaction to anyone with sensitive skin. Chrome is a relatively recent mordant, which was used in the woollen textile industry in Europe in the nineteenth century. Chrome allowed fast blacks to be dyed in two hours when it had previously taken two days. Chrome is sensitive to light and needs to be stored in a dark place. It encourages fast colours on all fibres.

Copper (copper sulphate)
As it comes in the form of turquoise crystals, copper is also known as 'blue copperas', 'blue-vitriol' or 'blue-stone'. This poisonous mordant was particularly important to the textile trade during the seventeenth and eighteenth centuries, though it had been in use as far back as the first century AD. It can be used on wool as a pre-mordant, or as an after mordant when it is used to sadden a colour. Copper gives a similar shade to chrome though the results are softer, duller and less intense. I found it had little effect on vegetable fibres.

Tin (stannous chloride)
Tin's white crystals are poisonous and an irritant. Tin was introduced into the textile industry in the seventeenth century, and gives a wonderful rich scarlet when used with cochineal on wool. When the mordant is used in the same bath as the dye, this colour is known as 'one-bath scarlet'. Used this way with madder, tin gives rich vibrant orange shades. On wool, tin can also be used as a pre-mordant or as an after mordant when it is added to the dye bath towards the end of the dyeing process. As an after mordant it is used to modify and brighten the colour. However, if too much tin is used on wool, it can make it brittle and affect its felting properties. This may be why the one-bath method is favoured as the dye seems to reduce the harshness. Tin is hardly ever used with vegetable fibres except in the dyeing of Turkey red, when tin crystals are added to the soap solution at the end of the dyeing process. The crystals help to brighten the red.

Iron (ferrous sulphate)

Since iron comes in the form of green crystals, it is sometimes known as 'green copperas' or 'green vitriol'. It can be harmful if ingested. Iron has been in use since the first century AD. Iron is used to create dark shades and often as an after mordant to sadden colours. It can also be used as a pre-mordant or in the one-bath method. Iron should be used in small quantities. If too much is used it can make wool brittle to touch and can be rather corrosive as seen in iron-mordanted brown and black shades in old rugs, which often degenerate with time. Scour the mordant bath thoroughly after use to ensure that no residue is left that may affect other colours in the future.

Tannic acid

This has a yellowish colour and is used as a pre-mordant as well as a fixing agent for vegetable fibres.

Mordant assistants

These are included in the recipes in this book for a variety of reasons:
- Acetic acid is used in conjunction with copper to improve its absorption and efficiency, and allows smaller amounts of copper to be used with better results.
- Cream of tartar (potassium hydrogen tartrate) brightens colours and improves the absorption of the alum mordant on animal fibres and helps keep wool soft.
- Formic acid is used in conjunction with chrome. The addition of formic acid helps chrome bond with wool and enables a more efficient take up of the mordant.
- Oxalic acid is generally used in conjunction with tin to give better results. It ensures an efficient take up and prevents superficial fixing of the mordant.

- Sodium carbonate (washing soda in crystal form or soda ash in powder form) is combined with alum to increase the alkalinity and facilitate the absorption of the mordant on vegetable fibres. It is also used in indigo and woad vats to increase the alkalinity and facilitate absorption.
- Sodium hydrosulphite (hydrotherm) is used to remove the oxygen from indigo and woad vats.
- Sodium phosphate is used once vegetable fibres have been treated with alum. It clears the fibre of surplus, unattached alum.

Making your own mordants

It is possible to make your own mordants, however, it is harder to control the amount of mordant you are using and record quantities and effects.

Plant mordants

Plants are a useful source of natural mordants. Oxalic acid is found naturally in rhubarb leaves (*Rheum* species), alum is found in clubmoss (*Lycopodium selago*) and tannin is found in oak galls (from the *Quercus* species) and sumac leaves (*Rhus typhina*).

To extract the mordant, experiment with soaking and boiling the ingredients in water, and then straining off the liquid before use. Be careful as some plants are harmful. Rhubarb leaves contain poisonous oxalic acid and when simmering a lid should be kept on the dye bath at all times. When estimating the amount of mordant, the general rule is to use the same weight of mordant material to the weight of yarn being dyed. I advise starting with wool.

Iron water

To make iron water, soak a handful of nails in a vinegar solution for a few days.

Disposal of chemical residues

- Advice should be sought from your public analyst or water authority. Ask them whether it is safe to dispose of spent mordants down the waste drain.
- Never dispose of spent mordants down the sink.
- Use only the amounts of chemicals advised in the recipes.
- Read the instructions on the packet or ask your supplier for advice. Disposal techniques will vary according to the chemical, as well as the area.
- Particular care needs to be taken when disposing of acids.
- Always add acid to water, *never* water to acid.
- Dilute concentrated acetic acid with water before disposing of it down the waste drain.
- Neutralize acid with household ammonia. The pH should read 6.5–7 before disposal.
- Before disposing of your dye bath containing sodium hydrosulphite, introduce oxygen into the dye bath by whisking air into it. This helps to use up the chemical before disposing of it down the drain.
- With chrome, Gill Dalby suggests using formic acid as an assistant, as it reduces the amount of mordant needed and encourages more of the mordant to attach itself to the fibre. This in turn exhausts the mordant bath and makes disposal safer and more efficient.

MORDANT RECIPES – ANIMAL FIBRES

All yarns must be fully scoured and wetted out before mordanting can begin (*see* p.20). Wool needs careful handling in order to prevent felting and shrinkage (*see* p.17). Although the yarn will need to be moved around the mordant bath, this must be done carefully, separating the skeins and opening them out, to avoid tangling and bunching. Handle mordants with care as some are toxic (*see* pp.22–5).

Alum

CHEMICAL INGREDIENTS

10% Alum

8% Cream of tartar

1 In a separate container, dissolve the alum and cream of tartar in a little hot water.

2 Add the solution to a cold mordant bath.

3 Enter the damp skein and bring the mordant bath to the boil in 1 hour.

4 Simmer gently for 1 hour.

5 Remove the skein.

6 Rinse well in hot water to ensure the removal of surplus, unfixed alum.

Chrome (*Based on a recipe by Gill Dalby*)

CHEMICAL INGREDIENTS

2% Chrome

4% Formic acid

1 Dissolve the chrome in a little hot water.

2 Add the solution to the cold mordant bath.

3 Enter the skein and bring to a gentle boil in 1 hour, keeping a lid on the mordant bath at all times. This contains toxic fumes and reduces the risk of uneven shades.

4 Simmer gently for 1 hour.

5 Do not allow the mordant bath to boil too vigorously as this adds unwanted air into the mordant bath. Since chrome is light-sensitive, if the light or air gets to the yarn

being mordanted, this may contribute to an uneven colour when the yarn is dyed.

6 Remove the skein quickly and carefully, trying not to expose it to the light.

7 Rinse well in hot water to ensure the removal of surplus, unfixed chrome.

8 Use the skein at once, or keep covered with a lid until dyeing can take place.

Tin 1 (*Based on a SIAD recipe*)

CHEMICAL INGREDIENTS

4%–8% Tin (See *individual recipes in* PART TWO *for precise amount*)

4% Oxalic acid

1 Dissolve the tin and the oxalic acid in a little hot water using two separate containers.

2 Add the solutions to the cold mordant bath, or if using the the one-bath method, add the mordant to the prepared dye bath.

3 Enter the skein, making sure it is moved around carefully in the solution.

4 Bring the bath to a gentle boil in 1 hour making sure the yarn is constantly submerged. Keep the lid on the bath during dyeing to contain the fumes.

5 Simmer gently for 1 hour.

6 Remove the skein.

7 Rinse well in hot water to remove any surplus, unfixed mordant.

Tin 2

CHEMICAL INGREDIENTS

4% Tin

10% Oxalic acid

1 Dissolve the tin and the oxalic acid separately in a little hot water.

2 Add the solutions to the cold mordant bath, or if using the one-bath method, add the mordant to the prepared dye bath.

3 Enter the skein and bring to the boil in 1 hour. Keep the lid on the bath during mordanting to contain the fumes.

4 Simmer gently for 1 hour.

5 Remove the skein.

6 Rinse well in hot water to remove surplus, unfixed mordant.

Iron 1

CHEMICAL INGREDIENTS

1%–5% Iron (See *individual recipes in* PART TWO *for precise amount*)

5% Sodium hydrosulphite

1 Make the stock solution of iron in a separate container with 500ml of cold water.

2 Sprinkle 5% hydrosulphite over the surface of the water and wait 10 minutes for the oxygen to leave the water.

3 Enter the iron and wait for it to dissolve.

4 Fill the mordant bath with cold water.

5 Enter the iron water and stir.

6 Enter the previously dyed, unrinsed skein.

7 Raise the bath to a gentle boil in 30 minutes, keeping a lid on the bath to contain fumes.

8 Remove the skein when required shade

CALCULATING QUANTITIES ALL QUANTITIES ARE GIVEN FOR 100G OF YARN (DRY WEIGHT) AND USE 3–4 LITRES OF WATER, UNLESS STATED OTHERWISE. ENSURE THERE IS ENOUGH WATER TO COVER THE MATERIAL BEING MORDANTED, AND THAT THE MATERIAL CAN BE MOVED EASILY AROUND THE MORDANT BATH.

has been achieved. This could be any time after 1 minute if the colour is correct.

9 Rinse well in hot water.

10 Soap wash and rinse until clear.

Iron 2 (*One-bath method*)

CHEMICAL INGREDIENTS

1%–5% Iron (See *individual recipes in* PART TWO *for precise amount*)

5% Sodium hydrosulphite

1 Sprinkle 5% hydrosulphite over the surface of 500ml of water.

2 Wait 10 minutes for the oxygen to leave the water.

3 Enter the iron and wait for it to dissolve.

4 Remove the skein from the dye bath after 1 hour, 30 minutes.

5 Add the iron water to the dye bath and stir.

6 Enter the skein and continue to simmer gently for 30 minutes, or remove the skein when the required shade has been achieved. Keep the lid on the dye bath during dyeing to contain the fumes.

7 Rinse well in hot water.

8 Soap wash and rinse until clear.

Copper (*Based on a recipe by Gill Dalby*)

CHEMICAL INGREDIENTS

3% Copper

3% Acetic acid

1 In a measuring jug or beaker, dissolve the copper in a little hot water.

2 Add it to the cold dye bath and stir.

3 Add the acetic acid and stir.

4 Enter the skein and raise to a gentle boil in 1 hour. Keep the lid on the mordant bath during mordanting to contain the fumes.

5 Simmer gently for 1 hour.

6 Remove the skein.

7 Rinse well in hot water.

8 Use at once to avoid wetting out again before dyeing.

Copper

STEP 2 *Pour in the copper solution and stir*

STEP 4 *Heat the mordant*

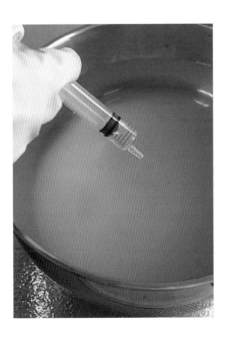

STEP 3 *Add the acetic acid with a syringe*

STEP 6 *Remove the skein*

MORDANT RECIPES – VEGETABLE FIBRES

Vegetable fibres take longer than animal fibres to prepare and usually need to be treated with tannic acid before mordanting and after scouring (*see* p.21). While indigo requires no mordant, indigo treated with tannic acid helps achieve some greens. For Turkey red, the yarn is steeped in oil and steamed before being treated with tannic acid. Handle mordants with care as many are toxic (*see* pp.22–5).

Tannic acid treatment 1 (*Based on a recipe by Ethel Mairet*)

CHEMICAL INGREDIENTS

5%–10% Tannic acid (*5% for the palest shade and 10% for the darkest shade*)

1 Dissolve the tannic acid in a little hot water and add it to the mordant bath.
2 Top up the mordant bath to 4 litres with cold water and stir well.
3 Enter the scoured skein and raise the temperature to 60 °C over 1 hour.
4 Maintain this temperature for 1 hour.
5 Leave the yarn in the mordant bath to cool overnight.

6 Reheat the mordant bath.
7 Remove the skein and rinse lightly.
8 Squeeze and mordant immediately whenever possible while the yarn is still damp.

Tannic acid treatment 2 (*Based on a recipe by Margaret Bide, SIAD*)

CHEMICAL INGREDIENTS

6% Tannic acid

1 Dissolve the tannic acid in a little warm water.
2 Add the solution to the mordant bath with 1.5 litres of water.
3 Stir well and raise the temperature of the mordant bath to 40 °C.
4 Enter the yarn and remove from the heat.
5 Leave the yarn to cool in the mordant bath overnight.
6 Remove the yarn and lightly rinse in warm water.
7 Squeeze and wherever possible mordant immediately while the yarn is still damp.
8 The yarn must be fully wetted out before mordanting.

Oil treatment (*Based on a recipe by Margaret Bide, SIAD*)

Traditionally this treatment is used to produce Turkey red.

CHEMICAL INGREDIENTS

Turkey red oil

28g Sodium phosphate per litre of water

1 Steep the yarn in Turkey red oil until the yarn is evenly saturated.
2 Squeeze out excess oil as evenly as possible and leave skein to dry. This is important since it helps to produce an even result.
3 Steam the dried, oiled yarn for 1 hour, 30 minutes under pressure, using a steamer, at a temperature of over 100 °C.
4 Repeat the oiling, drying and steaming several times to deepen the colour. (I did this three times.)
5 After oiling and steaming, apply tannic acid treatment 2.
6 Mordant with alum 2.
7 Rinse in a sodium phosphate solution using 10g to each litre of water.
8 Set the bath at 50 °C.
9 Immerse the skein for 10 minutes making sure that the skein is moved around evenly in the liquor.
10 The skein is now ready for dyeing.

Tannic acid treatment 1
STEP 5 *Soak yarn in tannic acid*

Yarn before and after treatment

Alum 1

CHEMICAL INGREDIENTS

50% Alum

1 Dissolve the alum in a little hot water.

2 Add the solution to the mordant bath.

3 Top up the mordant bath with cold water to 4 litres, stirring well.

4 Enter the damp tannic-acid-treated skein and move it around in the liquor.

5 Raise the temperature of the mordant bath to 60 °C over 1 hour.

6 Remove the mordant bath from the heat.

7 Leave the skein to soak overnight in the mordant bath.

8 Re-heat the bath the following day and leave to cool.

9 Rinse well in hot water to remove surplus, unfixed mordant just before dyeing commences.

Alum 2 (Based on a SIAD recipe)

This recipe, with the addition of soda ash followed by an ammonia solution rinse, produces darker shades more effectively than Alum 1.

CHEMICAL INGREDIENTS

200g Alum per litre of water

32g Soda ash per litre of water

50g Ammonia per litre of water

1 Dissolve the alum and soda ash separately in a little warm water.

2 Slowly mix the solutions together in the mordant bath with cold water. Stir gently to avoid excess frothing.

3 Set the bath at 40 °C.

4 Immerse the damp, tannic-acid-treated yarn and leave it to soak overnight.

5 Squeeze the yarn and leave it to dry.

6 Rinse well in a cold ammonia solution before dyeing.

Chrome (Based on a recipe from Natural Dyes for Vegetable Fibres by Gill Dalby)

CHEMICAL INGREDIENTS

1% Chrome

2% Formic acid

1 Dissolve the chrome in a little hot water and add it to the mordant bath.

2 Top up the mordant bath with cold water to 4 litres and stir well.

3 Using a syringe, add the formic acid carefully to the mordant bath and stir.

4 Enter the damp, tannic-acid-treated yarn. Cover with a lid immediately to keep out the light and contain fumes.

5 Raise the temperature to simmer, keep covered and simmer for 1 hour.

6 Leave the yarn in the bath to cool overnight and keep covered throughout.

7 Rinse well in hot water and dye immediately, taking care not to allow the air to get to the yarn as chrome is light sensitive. Light or air contact will cause the yarn to dye unevenly.

Copper (Based on a recipe from Natural Dyes for Vegetable Fibres by Gill Dalby)

CHEMICAL INGREDIENTS

2% Copper

2% Acetic acid

1 Dissolve the copper in a little hot water and add it to the mordant bath.

2 Top up the mordant bath with cold water to 4 litres and stir.

3 Enter the damp, tannic-acid-treated yarn and raise the temperature to a simmer.

4 Keep covered and simmer for 1 hour.

5 Leave the yarn in the mordant bath to cool overnight.

6 Rinse well in hot water to remove surplus, unfixed mordant and dye immediately.

Iron (Based on a recipe by Margaret Bide, SIAD)

CHEMICAL INGREDIENTS

0.5–2% Iron (See individual recipes in PART TWO for precise amount)

1 Dissolve iron in hot water and add to the mordant bath.

2 Top up the mordant bath with cold water to 4 litres and stir.

3 As an after mordant, enter the damp, previously dyed and unrinsed yarn.

4 Raise the temperature to simmer and keep covered. Simmer for 30 minutes or until the desired colour has been achieved.

5 Remove the yarn from the mordant bath before a skin has formed on the surface, as this will cause unevenness when dyeing.

6 Rinse in warm water, soap wash and rinse again until the rinsing water is clear.

7 Squeeze and leave to dry, preferably out of direct sunlight.

Tin

I experimented with this recipe, however, tin only proved really effective on vegetable fibres when it was used as a colour modifier in the production of Turkey red. (See Madder 2 recipe on p.36.)

CHEMICAL INGREDIENTS

7% Tin

8% Oxalic acid

1 Dissolve tin and oxalic acid separately.

2 Add to mordant bath and top up mordant bath to 4 litres and stir.

3 Enter the damp, tannic-acid-treated yarn.

4 Raise the temperature to a simmer.

5 Keep covered and simmer for 1 hour.

6 Leave the mordant bath to cool.

7 Remove the skein.

8 Rinse well in hot water.

CALCULATING QUANTITIES ALL QUANTITIES ARE GIVEN FOR 100G OF YARN (DRY WEIGHT) AND USE 3–4 LITRES OF WATER, UNLESS STATED OTHERWISE. ENSURE THERE IS ENOUGH WATER TO COVER THE MATERIAL BEING MORDANTED, AND THAT THE MATERIAL CAN BE MOVED EASILY AROUND THE MORDANT BATH.

DYES

While there are many sources of natural colour (*see* pp.32, 38–41), the colour charts in PART TWO use only five dyestuffs: two reds: cochineal and madder; one yellow: weld; one brown: cutch; and one blue: indigo. Madder, weld, indigo and cutch are all plant dyes, but cochineal is derived from insects. These dyes have been chosen not only for the strong colours they yield and their resilience to fading, but also for their relative fastness and availability. Other than weld, which comes from Europe, these dyestuffs are native to the tropical world. They all can be purchased from reputable suppliers (*see* p.100). Natural dyestuffs are organic substances, and the quality of the colours they produce may vary from batch to batch and year to year.

Types of dye

Natural dyes fall into three main categories:
- Substantive dyes are those that do not need a mordant to bind the dye to the fibre, such as cutch. There are relatively few substantive dyes.
- Additive dyes, or mordant dyes, need a mordant in order for the dye to bond with the fibre, such as madder, cochineal and weld. This is the most common type of dye.
- Vat dyes form the third category and include indigo and woad. These dyes are insoluble in water, and need to be dissolved in a vat with alkalis. Oxygen is removed by a chemical process called reduction. On contact with air (oxidation), the dyes become stable soluble compounds.

Applying the dye

Although animal and vegetable fibres need to be treated differently, these guidelines relate to both processes:

1 The skeins need to be wetted out thoroughly before mordanting or dyeing can begin, to reduce the chances of uneven dyeing results.

2 Never leave your yarn to dye on its own.

3 Check that the skeins have enough liquid and space to move around freely in the dye bath, making sure that they never rise out of the dye liquor for too long at a time.

4 Allow as much time as possible for dyeing to ensure full take up: slower and longer treatments often give better results and ensure that more of the dye is attached to the fibres.

5 Rinse thoroughly after dyeing to remove any surplus unfixed dye.

Dyeing animal fibres

When dyeing wool or many other animal fibres, remember that the fibres could shrink and felt together if they are not handled with sufficient care (*see* p.17). In order to preserve silk's lustre, use lower temperatures when heating the dye bath used to dye silk.

Dyeing vegetable fibres

It is more difficult to dye vegetable fibres than animal fibres. They are more resistant to taking up good strong colours (*see* colour matching on p.17). More time should be allowed for dyeing linen since it is even more resistant to taking up dye and takes longer to acquire depth of shade.

The dyestuffs

The colour charts in PART TWO represent something of the exciting range of colours that can be achieved through using a limited number of dyestuffs, combined with a variety of dyeing procedures (*see* panel on p.25). The procedure and order of dyeing will affect the colour you obtain. For example, indigo dyed over mordanted weld can give you yellow greens, whereas weld over dyed onto unmordanted indigo will give blue dominated greens.

Weld (*Reseda luteola*)

Weld, also known as dyer's rocket or dyer's weed, is a biennial herbaceous plant, native to Europe. It can also be found growing in western Asia, North Africa and North America. It can grow wild along the sides of motorways, chalk downland and on disturbed soil and gravel. All the plant except the root contains colouring matter, and it can be used fresh or dry. I still collect my own supply of weld around July and August. I harvest it into bundles, carefully drying it ready for storage and use until the following season.

Weld has been found in Neolithic settlements in Switzerland and in the Indus Valley dating as far back as 2,500 BC and, according to Pliny, it was used in Rome to dye wedding garments in the first century AD. It used to be cultivated as a dye crop in England and Europe and was prized as one of the oldest and fastest sources of yellow. In medieval England, it was used with woad and indigo to create greens such as Kendal green, Lincoln green and Saxon green. Following practices in America, weld was

1 *Fine indigo powder* **2** *Indigo grains* **3** *Cochineal* **4** *Ground cochineal* **5** *Cutch powder*
6 *Cutch resin* **7** *Madder powder* **8** *Best Turkish madder* **9** *Chopped root of madder*
10 *Dried weld plant* **11** *Chopped weld*

Sources of natural colour

There are many sources of natural colour:

- **Plants** are the richest source of natural dyes (*see* pp.38–41).
- **Lichens** have been a traditional source of dyes for at least two thousand years. Lichens should no longer be used as they are much rarer than they used to be due to the ill-effects of air pollution.
- **Shellfish** of the *Purpura* and *Murex* species produced Tyrian purple. From the ancient world to the mid-fifteenth century, Tyrian purple was the most revered colour, associated with high rank and royalty. In Oaxaca, Mexico, lilac-coloured cotton is still dyed with liquid secreted by molluscs (*Purpura patula*).
- **Minerals**, such as yellow ochre or red ochre, can be used for dyeing material.
- **Scaly insects** of several varieties yield a red to purple dye very similar to cochineal. They include:

Lac, an insect native to India, feeds mainly on acacia and fig trees. Its name means hundreds and thousands, indicating the large number of insects needed to produce the colour.

Kermes took the place of Tyrian or Imperial purple in the Middle Ages, with the collapse of the Byzantine Empire. Kermes could be found in Turkey, Armenia, around Mount Ararat, and Europe. Depending on the species, the insects live on oak leaves (*Quercus* species), or grasses and roots.

Poland supplied its own insect St John's Blood to Holland, Flanders, Venice and Florence, until Arab merchants supplied cochineal from Burma and Indochina.

superseded by fustic (*Chlorophora tinctoria*) and quercitron, derived from the inner bark of the oak tree *Quercus velutina*. Today, however, weld is still commonly used by the craft dyer. It yields bright yellows with alum and tin mordants, rich golden yellows to tobacco browns with a chrome mordant and greenish yellows with copper and iron mordants.

Madder *(Rubia tinctorum)*

Madder yields a range of reddish colours from pink to deep scarlet. The colouring matter of the madder plant is in its root, which takes a minimum of three years and up to seven years to mature. The root is dried and made into powder or chopped up. In my recipes I found the richest colours were achieved with what is called 'best Turkish madder'. Though there are several different species that can yield a dye, *Rubia tinctorum* is the most common species of madder used for dyeing. It is an herbaceous perenniel, which grows wild and thrives in well-drained, chalky soil. It is a native of India, the East and parts of Europe.

Evidence of madder-dyed cotton cloth has been found in the Indus Valley dating from around 3,000 BC as well as on linen cloth in Egyptian tombs. In the Middle Ages, madder red was much prized in Europe and was used for dyeing wedding clothes and other garments for special occasions. In Europe madder from Holland was regarded as the best quality madder until the nineteenth century.

Madder was highly valued as the chief ingredient of Turkey red, a rich, fast, bright red used for dyeing cotton mostly. It originated in India, where its recipe remained a closely guarded secret until it spread to Turkey. The original Turkey red took at least a month to complete, involving

sixteen different processes. Though Marco Polo was aware of it, the secret of Turkey red did not reach Europe until the seventeenth century, when Greece became a centre for Turkey red production. In 1747 Greek dyers brought the secret to Rouen, France. Other European countries, such as Germany and Britain, soon learnt how to produce Turkey red. There was a dramatic decline in the use of madder following the development of synthetic alizarin, the main pigment found in madder roots, by the French chemist Pierre Jean Robiquet in 1826. However, in France, natural madder was still used to dye military trousers up until World War I.

Cochineal *(Dactylopius species)*

Cochineal is a scaly insect from the Dactylopius family and formerly referred to as *Coccus cacti* or 'scarlet grain'. The female insect is used for dyeing after it has been carefully gathered and dried. The colouring matter carminic acid is found in the shell, though the whole insect is used. It is a parasitic insect which lives on the prickly pear cacti from the Opuntia and Nopalea family.

Cochineal originated from Central and South America, where it was used to dye carmine red by the native Indians as far back as 1,000 BC. The Spanish discovered it in Mexico in the sixteenth century and tried to keep it a secret, but by the end of the eighteenth century, cochineal cultivation had spread to Guatemala, Brazil and Java and later to the West Indies, Algeria and the Canary Islands. Cochineal was also found in Armenia, where it had been used as a dye since 800 BC. The Spanish eventually exported it from Armenia to Venice, Genoa and Marseilles. Because the cochineal insect is so small and has to be collected by hand by brushing the insects off their host plant, cochineal has always been an expensive dyestuff, a reserve of the rich. When used with a tin mordant, cochineal gives a rich vermilion red which was used for 'hunting pink' in Britain. Used with different mordants, cochineal produces a range of colours from grey to bright crimson and deep purple.

Indigo (Indigofera tinctoria)
Indigo blue comes from the fermented leaves of the genus *Indigofera*, native to India but cultivated throughout the tropical world. There are several species of *Indigofera*, *Indigofera tinctoria* being the most common.

Indigo was introduced into Europe in the sixteenth century, after Vasco da Gama discovered the sea route to India. At this time woad (*Isatis tinctoria*) was the main source of blue dye. Indigo did not take over from woad until the Dutch and Portuguese began importing it in huge quantities from India in the eighteenth century and swamped the market. Despite laws protecting the woad producers, indigo was so much more concentrated than woad, it very quickly took over as the best source of strong reliable blues.

Indigo is a vat dye. This means it is insoluble in water and needs to be deoxidized and dissolved in an alkaline solution before it can be absorbed. Indigo and woad contain a substance called indigotin, which is blue and insoluble. The blue dye is released from the leaves of the plant through an involved process of fermentation, the residue is then dried, formed into cakes and sold as a dye. Before 1900 and the use of sodium hydrosulphite (hydrotherm), the indigo vat was prepared using urine to deoxidize the indigo for

dyeing. This causes the vat solution to turn yellow in appearance, an indication to the dyer that dipping can commence. On entering the indigo vat, the fibre absorbs the indigo. On exposure to the air, indigo oxidizes and turns from yellow to green to blue. In order to build up a dark shade of blue, it is necessary to dip the fibres several times as the yarn can only absorb so much pigment at a time. Multiple dips also help to improve the evenness of shade, though this is notoriously difficult with indigo. Although indigo is fast to light, the dye does rub away because it is deposited in layers.

Indigo is not only good for supplying an excellent range of blues, it is also useful for over dyeing and under dyeing to create compound colour mixtures such as greens, greys and purples.

Cutch (Acacia catechu)
This dye is extracted from the heartwood of the *Acacia catachu* tree through boiling up the heartwood and reducing the liquid to a resin which is dried and either sold in lumps or ground into a powder.

Acacia catechu is a deciduous tree. It is native to India, Burma and Sri Lanka but it grows in many other tropical regions. Cutch originated from India where it was used in the calico printing trade long before it was known in Europe. Exported to China and Japan in the sixteenth century, it was for a time called *Terra japonica*, Japanese earth, since it was thought to be a mineral dye from Japan. Cutch was first used in Europe in the nineteenth century and was the last important vegetable dye to be added to the professional dyers' reper-toire. It yields warm browns, and combined with indigo it is useful for obtaining greys. Although it is a substantive dye, a mordant can improve the colour and fastness.

Extending the colour range

There are a variety of ways to extend your colour range:
• **Different mordants** can radically alter the end result. For example, cochineal on wool can be dyed a bright crimson with a tin mordant, a rich plum red with an alum mordant, a deep purple with a chrome mordant and grey with an iron mordant.
• **After mordants** and other substances can modify the colours you have dyed already. Iron is often used to sadden a colour, while tin is used to brighten one.
• **Mixing two dyestuffs** in the same dye bath. For example recipes 22–4 (*see* p.72) combine weld and cochineal in varying proportions to produce a range of orange shades.
• **Over dyeing** one colour on top of another. By over dyeing it is possible to create greens with weld and indigo for instance.
• **Exhaust dyeing** is when a dye is used more than once. First exhaust means the second dyeing, second exhaust refers to the third dyeing, this can literally go on until there is no dye left in the dye bath. This produces a series of paler shades, which are often thought to be less light fast than the colours obtained from the fresh dye bath (*see* pp.56–7).
• **The water pH** can alter a colour. A more vibrant orange would have been achieved on p.49 with more acidic water.
• **The quality** of the actual dyestuff is another influencing factor. On pp.49–50 the quality of the madder dyestuff is very influential in the final colour.

DYE RECIPES – ANIMAL FIBRES

All yarn must be fully scoured (*see* p.20), mordanted (*see* pp.26–7) and wetted out before dyeing. The times suggested below are the minimum times required; slower and longer treatments yield better results. As wool is prone to felting and shrinkage (*see* p.17), check the temperature regularly and give an occasional gentle stir to ensure that the heat is evenly distributed throughout the dye bath.

Cochineal

PREPARATION OF DYESTUFF

1 Grind the cochineal into a powder with a pestle and mortar or coffee grinder.
2 Place the cochineal powder in the dye bath with 1 litre of water.
3 Heat to leach out the dye.
4 Top up the dye bath with 3 litres of cold water, or enough to cover the yarn, and stir.

DYEING

5 Enter the damp, mordanted skein.
6 Raise the temperature of the dye bath to boil in 1 hour.
7 Simmer gently for 1 hour.
8 Allow the bath to cool, remove the skein.
9 Rinse thoroughly in warm water.
10 Spin and leave to dry naturally.

Cutch

PREPARATION OF DYESTUFF

1 Mix the cutch powder into a paste with a little cold water and place the paste in the dye bath. If resin is being used, dissolve resin in 1 litre of hot water.
2 Top up the dye bath with about 3 litres of cold water.

DYEING

3 Enter the damp, mordanted skein.
4 Raise the temperature of the dye bath to boil in 1 hour.

5 Simmer gently for 1 hour.
6 Allow the bath to cool, remove the skein.
7 Rinse thoroughly in warm water.
8 Spin and leave to dry naturally.

Indigo (*Based on a SIAD recipe*)

Wear a face mask while preparing this recipe as well as your overall and gloves.

INGREDIENTS FOR THE STOCK SOLUTION

5g Indigo
5g Caustic soda
10g Sodium hydrosulphite

PREPARATION OF INDIGO VAT

1 Mix indigo into a paste to dissolve with a little hot water.
2 Place the paste into a stainless steel pan with 375ml of cold water.
3 Put 125ml of cold water into a glass measuring jug and add the caustic soda. Stir until the water turns clear.

Always add caustic soda to cold water, *never* add water to caustic soda.

4 Add the caustic soda solution to the indigo stock.
5 Sprinkle the sodium hydrosulphite onto the surface of the stock solution.
6 Place the stock pan into a bowl of water, to act like a double saucepan.
7 Raise the temperature of stock to 60 °C for 20 minutes, taking care not to overheat

the solution as indigo is destroyed at 76 °C.
8 The solution should show as a clear yellow turning to blue in seconds.
9 If white spots occur, add more caustic soda solution. If blue spots occur, add more sodium hydrosulphite.

DYEING

10 Fill the dye bath with hot water.
11 Sprinkle hydrosulphite onto the surface.
12 Raise the temperature to 50 °C and wait 10 minutes. For pale shades you can use an almost cold bath; this slows down the dyeing action and gives a more even result.
13 Add a small amount of dye stock, a little at a time, taking care to note the exact amount for recording purposes.
14 Move aside the skin that forms on the surface of the dye bath.
15 Carefully enter the damp, lightly soaped and rinsed skein, taking care not to add any oxygen to the bath.
16 Leave for a few minutes, making sure to record the time and the number of dips.
17 For every minute the yarn remains in the bath, allow a minimum of the same amount of time out of the bath for oxidation.
18 Separate the skein to allow the air to penetrate fully.
19 Rinse thoroughly in warm water.
20 Steep in acid water (3.5ml of acetic acid to 15 litres of water) for 10 minutes to neutralize the caustic soda.
21 Rinse, and scour thoroughly. Delay final scouring for a few days for darker shades. An addition of ammonia gives a redder blue, while an addition of salt dissolved in hot water helps to exhaust the dye bath.

CALCULATING QUANTITIES ALL QUANTITIES ARE GIVEN FOR 100G OF YARN (DRY WEIGHT); DYESTUFF AMOUNTS ARE GIVEN IN PART TWO. USE 3–4 LITRES OF WATER, UNLESS STATED OTHERWISE. ENSURE THERE IS ENOUGH WATER TO COVER THE MATERIAL BEING DYED, AND THAT IT CAN BE MOVED EASILY AROUND THE DYE BATH.

34 DYE RECIPES

Weld

PREPARATION OF DYESTUFF

1 Place the chopped weld in the dye bath with 1 litre of water.

2 Heat until the colour leaches out into the water.

3 With cold water, top up the dye bath to 4 litres.

DYEING

4 Enter the damp, mordanted skein.

5 Raise the temperature of dye bath to boil in 1 hour.

6 Simmer gently for 1 hour.

7 Allow the bath to cool.

8 Remove the skein and hand-wring.

9 Shake the skein to remove dye material.

10 Rinse thoroughly in warm water.

11 Spin and leave to dry naturally.

Madder

PREPARATION OF DYESTUFF

1 Sprinkle the powdered madder into a cold dye bath stirring continuously to avoid lumping, or mix powder into a paste with a little cold water and add this to the cold dye bath. If chopped madder root is used, place the slithers into a dye bath with 1 litre of cold water and heat gently until the colour leaches out into the water, being careful not to boil the madder. Allow to cool.

2 With cold water, top up the dye bath to 4 litres.

DYEING

3 Enter the damp, mordanted skein and raise the temperature to simmer in 1 hour.

4 Simmer for 1 hour. Do not allow madder to boil as this gives the colour a dull yellow tinge that cannot be reversed.

5 Allow bath to cool and remove the skein.

6 Hand-wring and shake the skein to remove excess dye material.

7 Rinse thoroughly in warm water, spin and leave to dry naturally.

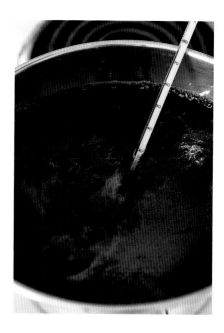

Madder

STEP 1 *Off the hob, stir madder powder continuously to avoid lumping*

STEP 3 *After adding skein, gently heal dye bath, raising to a simmer in 1 hour*

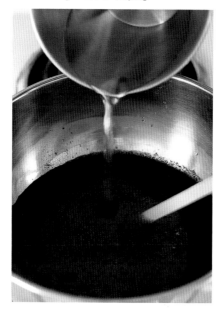

STEP 2 *Top up dye bath with cold water*

STEP 5 *Allow bath to cool and remove skein*

DYE RECIPES – VEGETABLE FIBRES

Vegetable fibres are more resistant to taking up good strong colours and need to be scoured (see p.21), mordanted (see pp.28–9) and thoroughly wetted out before dyeing can begin, to reduce the chances of uneven dyeing. Since vegetable fibres need time to become fully saturated, it is easier to mordant immediately after scouring, and dye straight after mordanting. However, as the processes are rather lengthy, this may not always be possible. The times suggested below are a minimum: the slower and longer the treatment, the better the end result. It is important to bear in mind that after dyeing and rinsing, the colour on vegetable fibres will dry at least fifty per cent paler than it appears when damp.

Madder 1

PREPARATION OF DYESTUFF

1 Place the slithers of chopped madder root in the dye bath with 1 litre of water. Heat to leach out dye, and with cold water, top up the bath to 4 litres. If madder powder is used, mix it into a paste with a little cold water before adding it to the dye bath.

DYEING

2 Enter the damp, mordanted skein.
3 Raise the temperature from cold to boiling point in 1 hour.
4 Gently simmer for 1 hour, making sure that the yarn is constantly submerged.
5 Carefully move the skein around in the dye liquor to ensure even distribution of heat and dye.
6 For deeper shades simmer longer, topping up with water when necessary.
7 Leave to cool overnight.
8 Reheat the dye bath and leave to cool.
9 Remove the skein from the dye bath.
10 Hand-wring and shake out surplus dye material.
11 Rinse in hot water until the water is clear, wash in soap and rinse.
12 Allow to dry naturally out of direct sunlight.

Madder 2 *(Based on a SIAD recipe)*

This recipe is used for Turkey red.

BEFORE DYEING

1 Treat the skein with Turkey red oil (see p.28). When I was dyeing the Turkey red colours (see shades 43–51 on p.76), I oiled and steamed the skein three times, which took three days using a galvanized metal mesh basket on top of a dye bath with water and a lid on top to keep in the steam.
2 Treat the skein with tannic acid treatment 2 (see p.28).
3 Mordant the skein with alum (see p.29).

PREPARATION OF DYESTUFF

4 Use the same procedure as in the recipe for madder 1.

DYEING

5 Enter the damp, mordanted skein.
6 Raise the temperature from cold to 70°C slowly.
7 Keep at 70 °C for 2–4 hours, the longer the treatment the better.
8 Hand-wring, and shake out surplus madder.
9 Rinse in hot water until water is clear.
10 Boil in a soap solution for 10 minutes, using 10g of soap flakes per litre of water. Allow enough solution to adequately cover the yarn.
11 Add 0.15% tin crystals to the soap solution. It is not vital to add tin but it helps to brighten the colour. Be careful not to use too much as it creates insoluble tin-soap, which adheres to the yarn and ruins it.
12 The colour should turn from rust brown to red during the soaping process.
13 Rinse until the water is clear.
14 Allow to dry naturally out of direct sunlight.

Cochineal

PREPARATION OF DYESTUFF

1 Grind the cochineal in a pestle and mortar, or use a coffee grinder.
2 Place the cochineal powder in a dye bath with 1 litre of water, and heat to leach out the dye.
3 Top up the bath with 3 litres of cold water.

DYEING:

4 Enter the damp, mordanted yarn.
5 Raise the temperature to the boil in 1 hour.
6 Simmer for 1 hour.
7 Leave to cool overnight.
8 Reheat dye bath and then leave to cool.
9 Hand-wring and rinse in hot water until the water is clear.

CALCULATING QUANTITIES ALL QUANTITIES ARE GIVEN FOR 100G OF YARN (DRY WEIGHT); DYESTUFF AMOUNTS ARE GIVEN IN PART TWO. USE 3–4 LITRES OF WATER, UNLESS STATED OTHERWISE. ENSURE THERE IS ENOUGH WATER TO COVER THE MATERIAL BEING DYED, AND THAT IT CAN BE MOVED EASILY AROUND THE DYE BATH.

10 Wash the yarn in soap (using 5g of soap flakes per litre of water).

11 Rinse in hot water, hand-wring or spin dry or leave to dry naturally.

Weld

PREPARATION OF DYESTUFF

1 Place the broken up or chopped weld in a dye bath with 1 litre of hot water.

2 Heat until the colour leaches into the water.

3 Top up the dye bath with enough water to cover the yarn.

DYEING

4 Enter the damp, mordanted yarn into the cold dye bath and raise the temperature slowly to the boil in 1 hour.

5 Gently simmer for 1 hour.

6 Allow the dye bath to cool overnight.

7 Remove the yarn, hand-wring and shake out surplus dyestuff.

8 Rinse in hot water until the water is clear.

9 Wash with soap (using 5g of soap flakes per litre) before final rinsing.

10 Hand-wring or spin.

11 Leave to dry naturally.

Cutch

PREPARATION OF DYESTUFF

1 Mix the cutch powder into a paste with a little cold water before adding it to the dye bath with 4 litres of cold water or enough to cover the yarn to be dyed. If resin is being used, dissolve the resin in 1 litre of hot water.

DYEING

2 Enter the damp yarn into the cold dye bath and raise the temperature slowly to the boil in 1 hour.

3 Gently simmer for 1 hour.

4 Allow the dye bath to cool overnight, remove the yarn and hand-wring, or spin.

5 Rinse until the water is clear.

6 Wash with soap (using 5g of soap per litre) before final rinsing.

7 Hand-wring or spin, and leave to dry naturally out of direct sunlight.

...o (Based on a SIAD recipe)

INGREDIENTS FOR INDIGO STOCK

50g Salt

0.25–8g Indigo

3.3g Caustic soda

10g Sodium hydrosulphite

PREPARATION OF INDIGO VAT

1 Fill the dye bath with 3 litres of water at 21 °C.

2 Add 50g of salt.

3 Add 3.3g of caustic soda to 28ml of cold water. Stir until dissolved.

4 Add the solution to the dye bath.

5 Sprinkle 10g of sodium hydrosulphite onto the surface of dye bath and stir it in.

6 Add the indigo grains to the dye bath, a little at a time, stirring gently to avoid adding oxygen to the bath.

7 Allow to stand for 2 hours before using.

DYEING

8 Enter damp skein into dye bath, gently to avoid adding air to the bath.

9 Leave under the surface from 30 seconds to 1 minute, 30 seconds.

10 Remove the skein carefully, avoiding adding air to dye bath.

11 Allow to oxidize for 3–5 minutes or until the all-yellow colour has turned blue.

12 Separate the skein to allow oxidation to penetrate fully.

13 To achieve deeper shades, repeat the process until the required depth of shade has been reached.

14 Hang in the air for as long as possible.

15 Rinse in cold water.

16 Wash in hot, soapy water.

17 Rinse in hot water and dry naturally out of direct sunlight.

Some useful technical terms

Additive dyes dyes that need a mordant to act as a fixative.

After mordant to mordant after dyeing.

Boiling off to clean by boiling in an alkali solution, made with sodium carbonate for cotton and linen fibres and soap flakes for silk.

Exhaust dye to re-use a dye bath.

Mordant a substance that combines with a dyestuff to form an insoluble compound, which fixes colour to a fibre.

Mordant assistants additions to the mordant bath that ensure more efficient absorption of the mordant by the fibre.

One-bath method mordant and dye are combined together in the same bath.

One-bath scarlet tin and cochineal are combined in the same bath for dyeing wool and other protein fibres.

Pre-mordant the fibres being dyed are mordanted before dyeing.

Raise to the boil heat from cold to boiling point over a period of time, usually 1 hour.

Skein loosely coiled bundle of yarn or thread.

Soaping process to boil off in soap. It is used for Turkey red, to clear the oil and bring out the colour.

Substantive dyes dyes such as cutch, lichens, alder bark and walnut hulls that need no mordant. They have a natural affinity with the fibres being dyed.

Vat dye dyes, such as indigo and woad, are vat dyes. They need an oxygen-free environment before the colour is able to attach itself to the fibre.

Wetting out to ensure the yarn or material is fully saturated with water.

HEDGEROW DYES

Most of this book is devoted to the use of classic dyestuffs because they yield the strongest colours and in the main, the fastest. They are mostly native to the tropical regions of the world. However, before the establishment of reliable trade routes, all colours were restricted to local regions. It was possible in Scotland, for instance, to recognize Highlanders from Lowlanders by the colours of the cloths they wore, and in India to this day it is possible to recognize where people come from by the colours they use. The colours may now be synthetic but they emulate those made from locally found dye materials. For the craft dyer who does not wish to purchase imported dyestuff, there is an abundance of choice.

Colour fastness

Almost any plant will yield some sort of colour. Most of the results will be variations on yellow, and a good many of the plants will yield softer, paler shades that may not be as fast as the classic dyestuffs. However, if the colours do fade, they will mostly fade gracefully and retain a harmony with each other, which cannot always be said of synthetic dyes.

Plant parts

Dyestuffs can be made from different parts of a plant, such as roots, leaves, bark, berries and flowers – each producing a particular colour. The fastness depends on the plant, but berries are particularly fugitive. In order not to disturb nature, it is crucial to develop an understanding of the natural habitat and growing patterns of the plants we wish to harvest. For example, weld is a biennial that produces flowering spikes in its second year of growth. If weld is gathered after the plant has flowered and after the seeds have turned black, the simple act of gathering will scatter the seeds and contribute to next year's growth.

Conservation

Many wild plants are protected. It is illegal to pick rare species and an offence to uproot any wild plants without the landowner's permission. If a plant is plentiful and robust, a simple rule of thumb is never to take more than ten per cent of the plant you are gathering. Always find out how vulnerable a species is before touching it at all. Sometimes any disturbance is too much. When collecting tree bark, care should be taken not to damage the tree. It is better to use prunings or bark from felled trees as trees may die once the bark has been removed from the living trunk.

If you are intending to dye large amounts, you must consider growing your own plants and allowing nature to continue unhindered. It is possible to grow many of the plants listed on the following pages.

Under threat

Lichens are a traditional source of natural colour, and were used in the production of Harris tweeds in Scotland well into the twentieth century. Lichens are made up of two separate organisms, a fungus and an algae, living together in a symbiotic relationship. It is important not to gather lichens since they are particularly sensitive to pollution and their habitats are constantly being threatened by development. They are extremely hard to cultivate and take from up to fifty to a hundred years to grow to the size of an average hand.

Dyestuff quantities

It is safe to say that freshly gathered plants, flowers and bark would need to be used on a basis of 100% to the dry weight of yarn for animal fibres and 200% to the dry weight of yarn for vegetable fibres. This should give a strong shade though it is always advisable to test your colours first using small skeins.

Freezing or drying dyestuffs

You need to pick the plants in season. If you are unable to use them straight away, you may wish to freeze or dry them. As a rule, dry the plants out of direct sunlight. Move the material about regularly and dry in a way that allows the air to circulate freely. This will ensure that the material does not grow mould or rot. Once it is dry, it should be stored in paper bags out of direct sunlight and in a dry, airy place.

Keeping records

Always label the dyestuffs clearly stating the date, what it is and giving information about where and when the material was gathered. Such factors as the time of picking and the various minerals in the soil can have an effect on the colours a plant yields, so meticulous recording may explain certain results.

MAKING PLANT DYES

For those wishing to use their own plant dyestuffs, it is important to record when, where and what was harvested, whether it was used fresh, dried or frozen, what percentage of dyestuff was used, what mordant was used, what order of mordanting and dyeing was followed and how long each process took. As with imported dyestuffs, the longer the yarn is kept in the dye, the darker the shade will be. The basic mordant and the dye recipes can be adapted using different ingredients. A rule of thumb for mordanting and dyeing is to raise to the boil over one hour and simmer for one hour. Vegetable fibres may require longer and are harder to dye. Personal experimentation is essential and can lead to some exciting results.

1 Slice the walnut husks and weigh.
2 Simmer in a little water to extract dye.
3 Strain the liquor and allow it to cool.
4 Top dye the bath up to 4 litres of water.
5 Enter the damp, mordanted yarn.
6 Raise to the boil in 1 hour.
7 Simmer for 1 hour.
8 Remove the yarn, rinse and dry.

Depth of shade

When dyeing with plant parts, I prefer to keep the dyestuff with the yarn, but you can also prepare the dyestuff first, strain it and use the liquor. This reduces the likelihood of uneven results, but will probably reduce the richness and depth of shade of the colour obtained.

Making a liquor

This example recipe uses walnuts from the black walnut tree (*Juglans nigra*), chosen for the fast browns it produces. It does not need a mordant, but alum improves the fastness. This recipe uses slices of frozen or fresh walnut husks, used at 100% strength for wool and 200% for cotton:

Extracting colour

While flowers and leaves just need to be simmered to extract colour, other plant parts may need special treatment. Berries and fruit should to be crushed and then strained to prevent particles escaping into the dye bath that could cause uneven dyeing. Berry dyes can be adversely affected by alkalis, such as soap. Bark and roots should be chopped and soaked for at least 24 hours, before being simmered to extract dye.

Walnut liquor
STEP 1 *Slice the walnut husks and weigh*

STEP 2 *Simmer until the colour leaches out*

STEP 3 *Strain the liquor*

HEDGEROW COLOURS

I have listed a selection of plants under the broad headings of reds, yellows, blues and browns, greys and blacks. The list is just meant to be a rough guide as you will find that the colours overlap, the reds may be orange-reds, pink-reds or purple-reds, with the yellows overlapping into oranges and greens. This is not a definitive list because almost every plant will yield some sort of colour. Dye materials can be gathered throughout the year, and here I give an idea of the harvesting times. The mordants will extend the range of colour potential and help to fix the dye in a more permanent state. I suggest you follow the mordant recipes previously discussed and experiment with wool skeins as wool is the easiest fibre to use.

Reds

Anchusa or Alkanet (*Alkanna tinctoria*)
Perennial with small blue flowers found in Europe and Britain.
Part used: dried roots, harvested in spring.
Alum as a mordant gives red-tan to purple-red.

Birch (*Betula* species)
Perennial commonly found in North America, Europe and Asia.
Part used: fresh inner bark, harvested all year round.
Alum as a mordant gives pink-red to purple.

Bloodroot (*Sanguinaria canadensis*)
Perennial found in moist woodland habitats, native to North America and Canada.
Part used: roots, harvested in winter.
Alum as a mordant gives red-orange. Tin as a mordant gives pinkish red.

Bramble (*Rubus* species)
Found in Britain and North America in woodlands and waste ground.
Part used: berries, harvested in late summer to early autumn.
Alum as a mordant gives rose pink.

Heather (*Calluna vulgaris*)
Hardy evergreen shrub found in Britain, Scandinavia and Asia Minor, especially in fresh peat.
Part used: fresh tips, harvested in mid to late summer.
The dye produces pink with no mordant.

Lady's bedstraw (*Galium verum*)
Found in North America and Europe, in particular Scotland.
Part used: roots, harvested in late autumn.
Chrome as a mordant gives a strong red. Alum and chrome as mordants give orange-red while chrome with iron as a mordant gives a purplish red.

Yellows

Agrimony (*Agrimonia eupatoria*)
Found in North America and north European grassy areas.
Part used: whole plant when fresh, harvested in spring.
Alum as a mordant gives yellow while chrome gives gold.

Barberry (*Berberis vulgaris*)
Perennial found in Europe and eastern Asia and North America.
Part used: bark from stems and root, harvested from autumn to winter.
Alum as a mordant gives a bright yellow, and tin gives a stronger yellow.

Birch (*Betula* species)
Commonly found in North America, Europe and Asia.
Part used: bark, collected all year round, or fresh leaves, harvested from late spring to early autumn.
Alum as a mordant with the leaf-dye gives yellow, while alum with the bark-dye gives a dull yellow to dull gold.

Bog myrtle or **Sweet gale** (*Myrica gale*)
Found in Scotland, Scandinavia and North America.
Part used: green leaves, harvested in late spring or early summer.
Copper as an after mordant gives a warm yellow brown; alum with tin as an after mordant gives an orange, while alum as the mordant with iron as the after mordant gives a yellow-green.

Broom (*Genista tinctoria*)
Found in North America, Europe and Scotland.
Part used: flowering tips, harvested in summer, and stems and young shoots, harvested in late spring.
Alum as a mordant gives a clear, bright yellow with the flower-dye, while it gives greenish yellow with the stem- or young

shoot-dye. Chrome as a mordant gives a deep yellow with the flower-dye and olive green with the young shoot-dye.

Buckthorn (*Rhamnus frangula* and *R. cathartica*)
Perennial found in Europe and stretches of North America.
Part used: berries, harvested from early summer to autumn, and bark, harvested all year round.
No mordant with the bark-dye produces brownish yellows. Berries with alum as a mordant give primrose yellow, while alum with cream of tartar gives a bright yellow and chrome gives a warm brown.

Dahlia (*Dahlia* species)
Garden flower found in most fertile temperate regions.
Part used: flower heads of brightly coloured varieties, harvested in summer.
Alum as a mordant gives a yellowish bronze-gold, while chrome produces an orange.

Dyer's chamomile (*Anthemis tinctoria*)
Perennial found in Europe, particularly the south and east, and North America.
Part used: flowerheads, harvested in summer.
Alum as a mordant gives a clear, golden-yellow, copper produces a greenish yellow and chrome gives a duller yellow.

Golden rod (*Solidago* species)
Perennial found in North America and Europe.
Part used: flower heads, harvested in summer.
Alum as a mordant gives a clear lemon-yellow to tan-yellow, while chrome as a mordant gives warm old gold.

Marigold (*Tagetes* species)
Found in Britain and native to Southwest America, Mexico and South America.
Part used: flower heads, harvested in summer.
Alum as a mordant gives a yellow, while chrome gives a golden yellow.

Ragwort (*Senecio jacobea*)
Found in Europe and North America.
Part used: whole upper part of plant, harvested in summer.
Alum as a mordant gives a strong yellow.

St John's wort (*Hypericum perforatum*)
Found in Europe and North America.
Part used: whole plant, but not root, harvested in summer.
Alum as a mordant gives a clear, medium yellow and chrome gives a buttercup yellow.

Blues
Elder (*Sambucus nigra*)
Perennial found in Europe.
Part used: berries, harvested in summer.
Alum as a mordant gives a violet. This is made bluer with an addition of salt.

Privet (*Ligustrum vulgare*)
Perennial found in Europe and North America.
Part used: fresh berries, harvested in autumn.
When combined with salt, alum as a mordant gives a blue.

Sloe (*Prunus communis*)
Perennial found in Europe, North America, Eurasia and parts of Asia.
Part used: fruit, harvested in autumn.
Alum as a mordant gives a grey-blue after a hot soap wash.

Woad or **Dyer's woad** (*Isatis tinctoria*)
Found in Europe and parts of Asia.
Part used: first-year leaves, used straight after gathering, from mid summer to mid autumn.
The dye gives good blues with no mordant, but alum gives a more striking blue.

Greys, blacks and browns
Alder (*Alnus* species)
Perennial found in Europe and North America.
Part used: bark, harvested all year.
Iron used as an after mordant gives grey-black. Alum gives yellow-brown.

Elder (*Sambucus* species)
Fast-growing, robust tree found in Europe and North America.
Part used: fresh bark, harvested all year round.
The dye gives a grey with no mordant. However, alum as a mordant gives brownish greys and iron as an after mordant produces a relatively deep grey.

Bramble (*Rubus* species)
Perennial found in Britain and America in woodlands and waste ground.
Part used: fresh, young shoots, harvested in spring.
Alum as a mordant gives a grey, alum combined with an iron after mordant gives a black to greyish purple.

Black walnut (*Juglans nigra*)
Perennial found in Europe and North America.
Part used: leaves, green outer husks, harvested in autumn.
No mordant or alum give brown, chrome produces dark brown and iron as an after mordant produces dark brown to black.

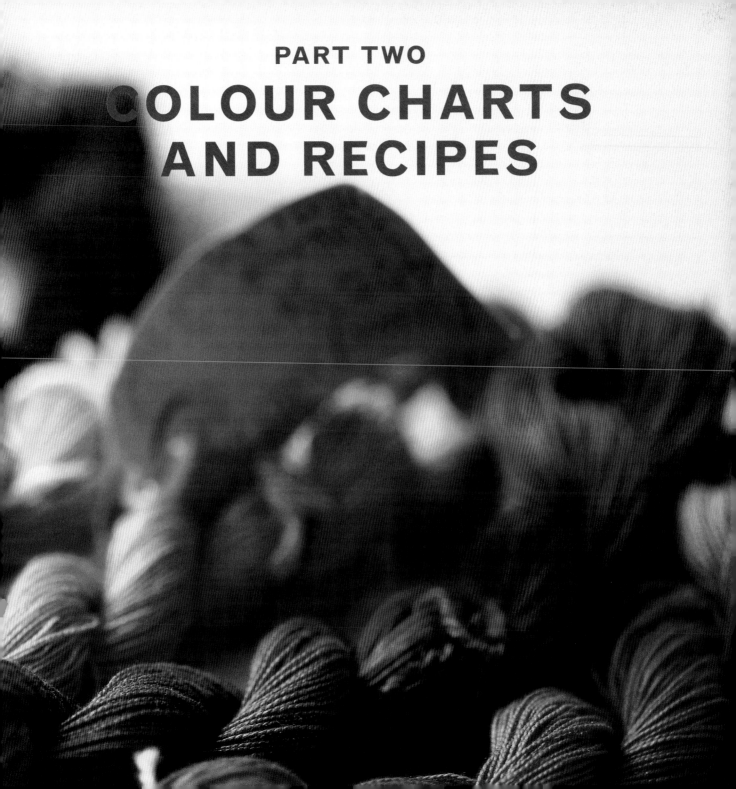

PART TWO
COLOUR CHARTS AND RECIPES

YELLOW – YELLOW-ORANGE RECIPES FOR ANIMAL FIBRES

These yellows are bright and vibrant with tin and alum mordants, but become duller with the addition of madder, resulting in burnt orange shades. Remember that different yarns will absorb the colour differently so testing is crucial to maintain control over your colours.

1

One bath – dye with mordant
Mordant: 8% Tin 1
Dye: 100% Weld

2

One bath – dye with mordant
Mordant: 6% Tin 1
Dye: 25% Weld

3

One bath – dye with mordant
Mordant: 4% Tin 1
Dye: 12.5% Weld

4

Pre-mordant: Alum
Dye: 25% Weld, *simmer for 1 extra hour*

5

Pre-mordant: Alum
Dye: 25% Weld

6

Pre-mordant: Alum
Dye: 12.5% Weld

7

Pre-mordant: Alum
Dye: 100% Weld, *simmer for 1 extra hour*

8

Pre-mordant: Alum
Dye: 100% Weld

9

Pre-mordant: Alum
Dye: 50% Weld

10

Pre-mordant: Alum
Dye: 12.5% Weld
Over dye 1: 0.25% Madder, *simmer for 30 min*
Over dye 2: 10% Weld, *simmer for 30 min*

11

Pre-mordant: Alum
Dye: 25% Weld
Over dye: 0.25% Madder, *simmer for 15 min*

12

Pre-mordant: Alum
Dye: 12.5% Weld
Over dye: Madder 1st exhaust from recipe 11, *simmer for 30 min*

13

Pre-mordant: Alum
Dye: 100% Weld
Over dye: 60% Cochineal, *leave yarn to cool in dye bath*

14

Pre-mordant: Alum
Dye: 100% Weld
Over dye: 5% Cochineal, *simmer for 1 hr*

15

Pre-mordant: Alum
Dye: 100% Weld
Over dye: Cochineal 1st exhaust from recipe 14, *simmer for 30 min*

16

Pre-mordant: Alum
Dye: 100% Weld
Over dye: 40% Cochineal, *leave yarn to cool in dye bath*

17

Pre-mordant: Alum
Dye: 50% Weld
Over dye: 10% Cochineal

18

Pre-mordant: Alum
Dye: 25% Weld
Over dye: 5% Cochineal

GOLD-YELLOW RECIPES FOR ANIMAL FIBRES

I was surprised how the addition of a second dye seemed to have a brownish effect on the colour whether I added cutch (brown dye) or cochineal (cerise dye) to the weld (yellow dye).

19
Pre-mordant: Chrome
Dye: 100% Weld

20
Pre-mordant: Chrome
Dye: 50% Weld

21
Pre-mordant: Chrome
Dye: 15% Weld

22
No mordant
Dye: 100% Weld

23
No mordant
Dye: 25% Weld

24
No mordant
Dye: 12.5% Weld

25
Pre-mordant: Alum
Dye: 7.5% Cochineal + 7.5% Weld

26
Pre-mordant: Alum
Dye: Cochineal 1st exhaust from recipe 25 + 7.5% Weld, *simmer for 1 hr 10 min*

27
Pre-mordant: Alum
Dye: Cochineal 2nd exhaust from recipe 27 + 7.5% Weld, *simmer for 45 min*

28
Pre-mordant: Alum
Dye: 100% Weld + 100% Cutch

29
Pre-mordant: Alum
Dye: 25% Weld + 25% Cutch

30
Pre-mordant: Alum
Dye: 15% Weld + 15% Cutch

31
One bath – dye with mordant
Mordant: 8% Tin 1
Dye: 100% Cutch

32
One bath – dye with mordant
Mordant: 6% Tin 1
Dye: 50% Cutch

33
One bath – dye with mordant
Mordant: 4% Tin 1
Dye: 25% Cutch

34
Pre-mordant: Chrome
Dye: 100% Weld, *leave yarn to cool in dye bath*

35
Pre-mordant: Chrome
Dye: 25% Weld, *leave yarn to cool in dye bath*

36
Pre-mordant: Chrome
Dye: 12.5% Weld, *leave yarn to cool in dye bath*

RECIPES: ALL RECIPES ARE BASED ON THE BASIC MORDANT AND DYE RECIPES IN PART ONE: MORDANTS *SEE* PP.26–7, DYES *SEE* PP.34–5. ANY VARIATIONS FROM THE BASIC RECIPES, OR STEPS PARTICULAR TO THE INDIVIDUAL RECIPE, ARE WRITTEN IN *ITALICS*.

QUANTITIES: ALL QUANTITIES ARE GIVEN FOR 100G OF YARN (DRY WEIGHT).   **WATER PH:** ALL RECIPES USE WATER PH 7 (*SEE* P.21).

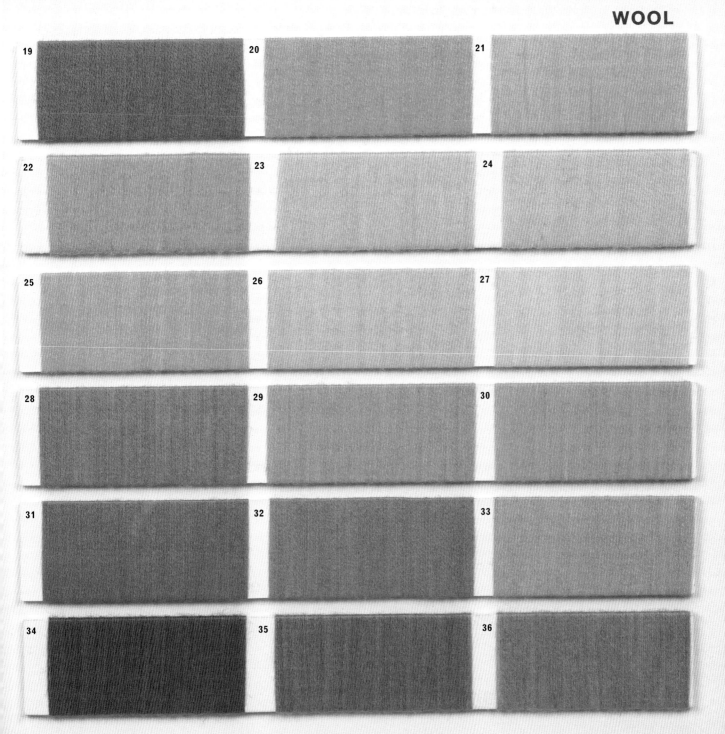

ORANGE – RED RECIPES FOR ANIMAL FIBRES

I used madder powder for recipes 40–2 and 46–8, and best Turkish madder for recipes 43–5 and 49–51. The superior quality of the best Turkish madder achieved a more dominant red. Though I was pleased with these shades, I still did not manage to obtain the particular vibrant orange I was looking for. An increased acidity might have given me a more intense and vibrant orange with a tin mordant.

37
Pre-mordant: Chrome
Dye: 100% Weld + 60% Cochineal

38
Pre-mordant: Chrome
Dye: 50% Weld + 30% Cochineal

39
Pre-mordant: Chrome
Dye: 12.5% Weld + 5 % Cochineal

40
Pre-mordant: Alum
Dye: 100% Weld + 100% Madder, *do not boil*

41
Pre-mordant: Alum
Dye: 50% Weld + 50% Madder, *do not boil*

42
Pre-mordant: Alum
Dye: 25% Weld + 25% Madder, *do not boil*

43
Pre-mordant: Alum
Dye: 100% Weld + 100% Madder, *do not boil; leave yarn to cool in dye bath*

44
Pre-mordant: Alum
Dye: 50% Weld + 50% Madder, *do not boil; leave yarn to cool in dye bath*

45
Pre-mordant: Alum
Dye: 25% Weld + 25% Madder, *do not boil; leave yarn to cool in dye bath*

46
Pre-mordant: Alum
Dye: 100% Madder

47
Pre-mordant: Alum
Dye: 50% Madder

48
Pre-mordant: Alum
Dye: 25% Madder

49
Pre-mordant: Alum
Dye: 100% Madder

50
Pre-mordant: Alum
Dye: 50% Madder

51
Pre-mordant: Alum
Dye: 25% Madder

52
One bath – dye with mordant
Mordant: Tin 2
Dye: 100% Madder + 60% Cochineal, *do not boil*

53
One bath – dye with mordant
Mordant: Tin 2
Dye: 50% Madder + 30% Cochineal, *do not boil*

54
One bath – dye with mordant
Mordant: Tin 2
Dye: 25% Madder + 15% Cochineal, *do not boil*

RECIPES: ALL RECIPES ARE BASED ON THE BASIC MORDANT AND DYE RECIPES IN PART ONE: MORDANTS *SEE* PP.26–7, DYES *SEE* PP.34–5. ANY VARIATIONS FROM THE BASIC RECIPES, OR STEPS PARTICULAR TO THE INDIVIDUAL RECIPE, ARE WRITTEN IN *ITALICS*.

QUANTITIES: ALL QUANTITIES ARE GIVEN FOR 100G OF YARN (DRY WEIGHT). WATER PH: ALL RECIPES USE WATER PH 7 (*SEE* P.21).

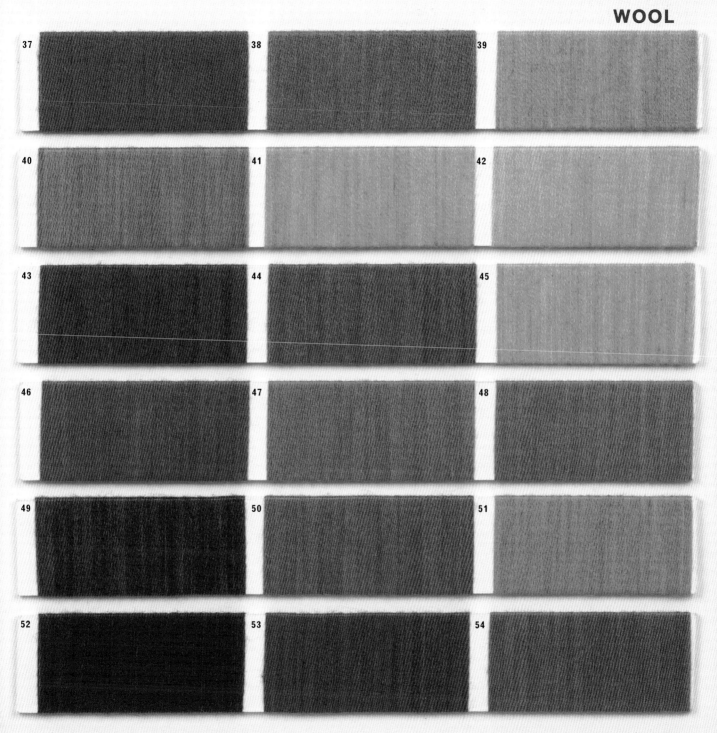

BROWN-RED – RED RECIPES FOR ANIMAL FIBRES

I used best Turkish madder for recipes 55–7. The colours in the last shade card of this set were dyed without a mordant, which gave a soft, pale range of shades. Mordants help to bring out as much depth in a shade as possible and yield more intense, stable colours.

55
One bath – dye with mordant
Mordant: 8% Tin 1
Dye: 100% Madder + 60%
Cochineal, *do not boil*

56
One bath – dye with mordant
Mordant: 6% Tin 1
Dye: 50% Madder + 30%
Cochineal, *do not boil*

57
One bath – dye with mordant
Mordant: 4% Tin 1
Dye: 25% Madder + 15%
Cochineal, *do not boil*

58
One bath – dye with mordant
Mordant: 8% Tin 1
Dye: 100% Madder
Over dye: 5ml Indigo stock,
5-min dip x 3

59
One bath – dye with mordant
Mordant: 6% Tin 1
Dye: 50% Madder
Over dye: 5ml Indigo stock,
5-min dip x 2

60
One bath – dye with mordant
Mordant: 4% Tin 1
Dye: 25% Madder
Over dye: 5ml Indigo stock,
5-min dip x 1

61
Pre-mordant: Alum
Dye: 100% Madder + 60%
Cochineal, *do not boil*

62
Pre-mordant: Alum
Dye: 50% Madder + 30%
Cochineal, *do not boil*

63
Pre-mordant: Alum
Dye: 25% Madder + 15%
Cochineal, *do not boil*

64
No mordant
Dye: 100% Madder

65
No mordant
Dye: 50% Madder

66
No mordant
Dye: 25% Madder

67
Pre-mordant: Chrome
Dye: 100% Madder

68
Pre-mordant: Chrome
Dye: 50% Madder

69
Pre-mordant: Chrome
Dye: 25% Madder

70
No mordant
Dye: 60% Cochineal + 100%
Weld

71
No mordant
Dye: 30% Cochineal + 50% Weld

72
No mordant
Dye: 15% Cochineal + 25% Weld

RECIPES: ALL RECIPES ARE BASED ON THE BASIC MORDANT AND DYE RECIPES IN PART ONE: MORDANTS *SEE* PP.26–7, DYES *SEE* PP.34–5.
ANY VARIATIONS FROM THE BASIC RECIPES, OR STEPS PARTICULAR TO THE INDIVIDUAL RECIPE, ARE WRITTEN IN *ITALICS*.
QUANTITIES: ALL QUANTITIES ARE GIVEN FOR 100G OF YARN (DRY WEIGHT).   WATER PH: ALL RECIPES USE WATER PH 7 (*SEE* P.21).

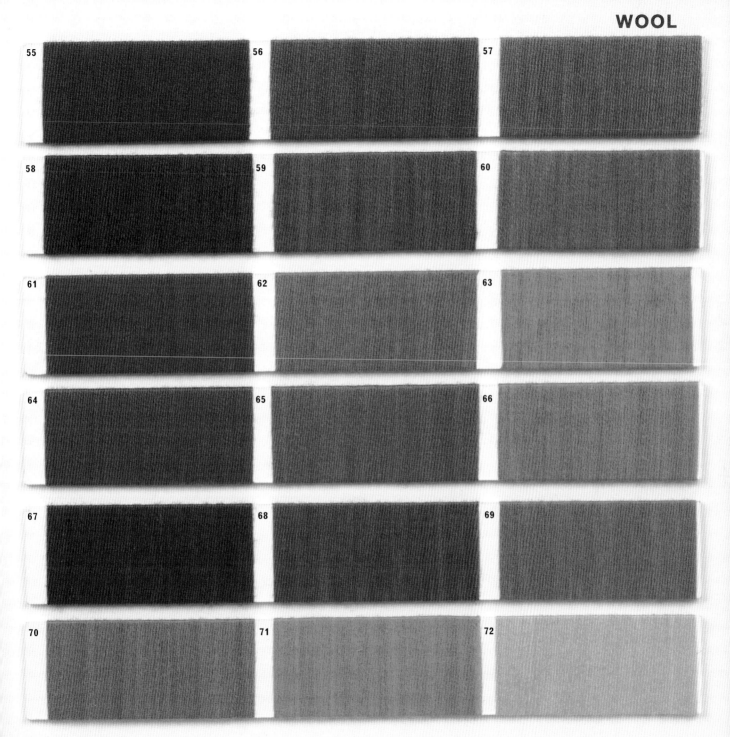

55
56
57
58
59
60
61
62
63
64
65
66
67
68
69
70
71
72

PINK – BROWN RECIPES FOR ANIMAL FIBRES

When using madder, I used madder powder, except for recipes 88–90 when I used best Turkish madder. When the recipe says cochineal + cutch this means the dyestuffs have been combined in the same dye bath, rather than applying one dye and then the other separately. This can affect the colour in ways you might not expect. Sometimes the colours seem to suppress each other and give less dramatic results.

73
Pre-mordant: Alum
Dye: 60% Cochineal + 30% Cutch

74
Pre-mordant: Alum
Dye: 30% Cochineal + 15% Cutch

75
Pre-mordant: Alum
Dye: 7% Cochineal + 3.5% Cutch

76
No mordant
Dye: 100% Madder + 40% Cochineal, *do not boil*

77
No mordant
Dye: 50% Madder + 20% Cochineal, *do not boil*

78
No mordant
Dye: 25% Madder + 10% Cochineal, *do not boil*

79
Pre-mordant: Chrome
Dye: 100% Madder + 60% Cochineal, *do not boil*

80
Pre-mordant: Chrome
Dye: 50% Madder + 30% Cochineal

81
Pre-mordant: Chrome
Dye: 25% Madder + 15% Cochineal, *do not boil*

82
No mordant
Dye: 100% Madder + 60% Cochineal, *do not boil*

83
No mordant
Dye: 50% Madder + 30% Cochineal, *do not boil*

84
No mordant
Dye: 25% Madder + 15% Cochineal, *do not boil*

85
Pre-mordant: Alum
Dye: 100% Madder + 60% Cochineal, *do not boil*

86
Pre-mordant: Alum
Dye: 25% Madder + 15% Cochineal, *do not boil*

87
Pre-mordant: Alum
Dye: 50% Madder + 30% Cochineal, *do not boil*

88
Pre-mordant: Chrome
Dye: 100% Madder + 60% Cochineal, *do not boil*

89
Pre-mordant: Chrome
Dye: 50% Madder + 30% Cochineal, *do not boil*

90
Pre-mordant: Chrome
Dye: 25% Madder + 15% Cochineal, *do not boil*

RECIPES: ALL RECIPES ARE BASED ON THE BASIC MORDANT AND DYE RECIPES IN PART ONE: MORDANTS *SEE* PP.26–7, DYES *SEE* PP.34–5. ANY VARIATIONS FROM THE BASIC RECIPES, OR STEPS PARTICULAR TO THE INDIVIDUAL RECIPE, ARE WRITTEN IN *ITALICS*.

QUANTITIES: ALL QUANTITIES ARE GIVEN FOR 100G OF YARN (DRY WEIGHT).   WATER PH: ALL RECIPES USE WATER PH 7 (*SEE* P.21).

73 74 75
76 77 78
79 80 81
82 83 84
85 86 87
88 89 90

BROWN RECIPES FOR ANIMAL FIBRES

These shades were achieved by using a range of dye and mordant combinations. Cutch is one of the few substantive dyes, which means that it has a natural affinity with wool and other animal fibres and does not need a mordant. However, mordants can be used to extend its colour range.

91
No mordant
Dye: 60% Cochineal +
100% Cutch

92
No mordant
Dye: 30% Cochineal +
50% Cutch

93
No mordant
Dye: 15% Cochineal +
25% Cutch

94
Pre-mordant: Copper
Dye: 100% Madder, *do not boil*

95
Pre-mordant: Copper
Dye: 50% Madder, *do not boil*

96
Pre-mordant: Copper
Dye: 25% Madder, *do not boil*

97
Pre-mordant: Chrome
Dye: 60% Cochineal +
100% Cutch

98
Pre-mordant: Chrome
Dye: 30% Cochineal +
50% Cutch

99
Pre-mordant: Chrome
Dye: 15% Cochineal +
25% Cutch

100
One bath – dye with mordant
Mordant: 3% Iron 1
Dye: 100% Madder, *do not boil*

101
One bath – dye with mordant
Mordant: 2% Iron 1
Dye: 50% Madder, *do not boil*

102
One bath – dye with mordant
Mordant: 1% Iron 1
Dye: 25% Madder, *do not boil*

103
Pre-mordant: Chrome
Dye: 100% Madder + 100% Weld,
do not boil

104
Pre-mordant: Chrome
Dye: 50% Madder + 50% Weld,
do not boil

105
Pre-mordant: Chrome
Dye: 25% Madder + 25% Weld,
do not boil

106
Pre-mordant: Alum
Dye: 100% Cutch

107
Pre-mordant: Alum
Dye: 50% Cutch

108
Pre-mordant: Alum
Dye: 25% Cutch

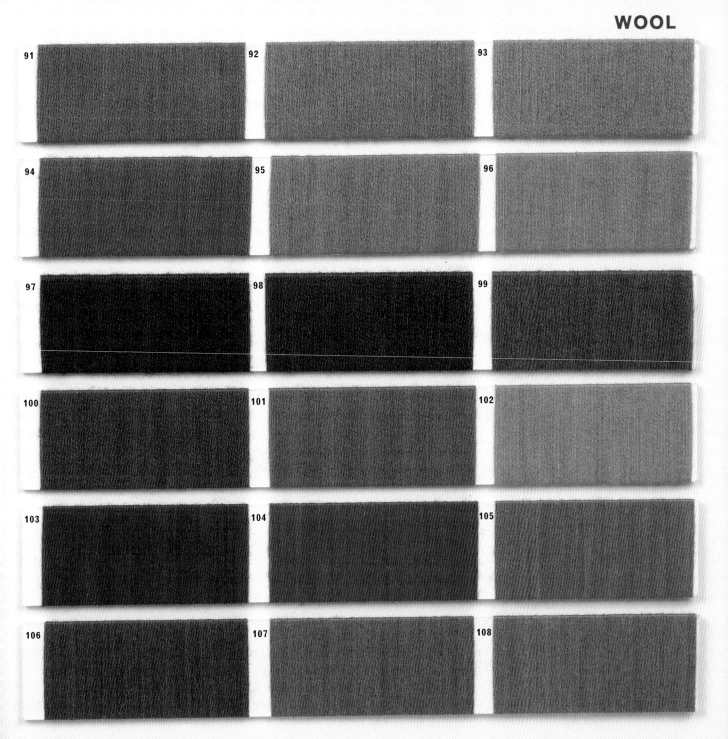

91 92 93
94 95 96
97 98 99
100 101 102
103 104 105
106 107 108

PINK – CRIMSON RECIPES FOR ANIMAL FIBRES

Exhaust cochineal takes on a yellowish tinge as it gets paler and paler with each successive dyeing. The alum skeins in 124–6 bring back the blueish pink quality of the colour while retaining some of the brightness and intensity.

109
Pre-mordant: Alum
Dye: Cochineal 1st exhaust
from recipe 114

110
Pre-mordant: Alum
Dye: Cochineal 2nd exhaust
from recipe 114

111
Pre-mordant: Alum
Dye: 10% Cochineal 3rd exhaust
from recipe 114

112
Pre-mordant: Alum
Dye: 40% Cochineal

113
Pre-mordant: Alum
Dye: 20% Cochineal

114
Pre-mordant: Alum
Dye: 10% Cochineal

115
One bath – dye with mordant
Mordant: 8% Tin 1
Dye: 60% Cochineal +
100% Weld

116
One bath – dye with mordant
Mordant: 6% Tin 1
Dye: 30% Cochineal + 50% Weld

117
One bath – dye with mordant
Mordant: 4% Tin 1
Dye: 7.5% Cochineal +
12.5% Weld

118
One bath – dye with mordant
Mordant: Tin 2
Dye: 60% Cochineal

119
One bath – dye with mordant
Mordant: Tin 2
Dye: 40% Cochineal

120
One bath – dye with mordant
Mordant: Tin 2
Dye: 30% Cochineal

121
One bath – dye with mordant
Mordant: 8% Tin 1
Dye: 40% Cochineal

122
One bath – dye with mordant
Mordant: 6% Tin 1
Dye: 20% Cochineal

123
One bath – dye with mordant
Mordant: 4% Tin 1
Dye: 10% Cochineal

124
Pre-mordant: Alum
One bath – dye with mordant
Mordant: 4% Tin 1
Dye: Cochineal 1st exhaust
from recipe 123

125
Pre-mordant: Alum
One bath – dye with mordant
Mordant: Tin 1
Dye: Cochineal 1st exhaust
from recipe 122

126
Pre-mordant: Alum
One bath – dye with mordant
Mordant: Tin 1
Dye: 5% Cochineal 2nd exhaust

RECIPES: ALL RECIPES ARE BASED ON THE BASIC MORDANT AND DYE RECIPES IN PART ONE: MORDANTS *SEE* PP.26–7, DYES *SEE* PP.34–5. ANY VARIATIONS FROM THE BASIC RECIPES, OR STEPS PARTICULAR TO THE INDIVIDUAL RECIPE, ARE WRITTEN IN *ITALICS*.

QUANTITIES: ALL QUANTITIES ARE GIVEN FOR 100G OF YARN (DRY WEIGHT). **WATER PH:** ALL RECIPES USE WATER PH 7 (*SEE* P.21).

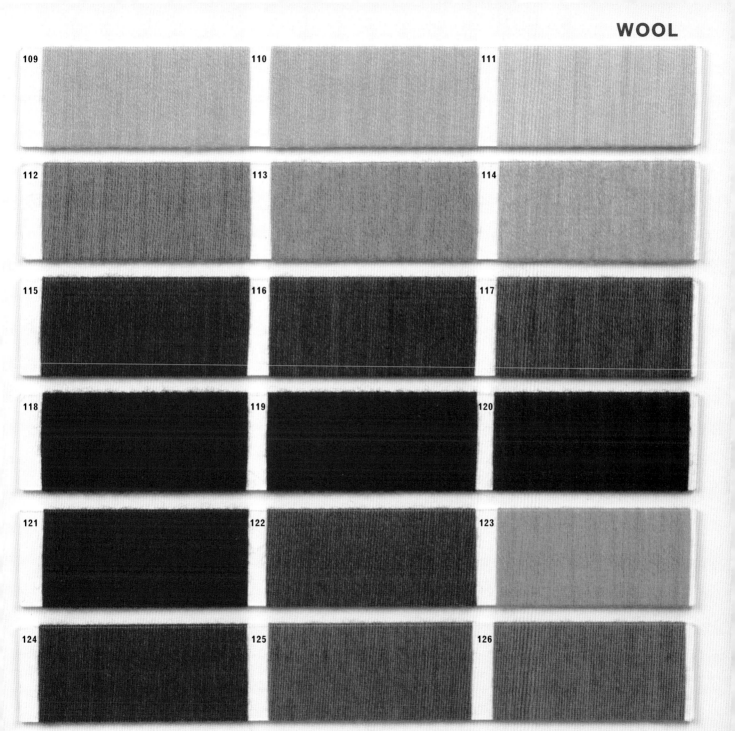

109 110 111
112 113 114
115 116 117
118 119 120
121 122 123
124 125 126

PALE VIOLET – RED-VIOLET RECIPES FOR ANIMAL FIBRES

Cochineal without a mordant gives an interesting colour but, as you will see, the range of violets possible is greatly extended by varying the mordant and using indigo as an over dye. You can experiment by varying the length of dip in the indigo as well as varying the concentration of the indigo bath.

127
No mordant
Dye: 6% Cochineal

128
No mordant
Dye: 3% Cochineal

129
No mordant
Dye: 1.5% Cochineal

130
No mordant
Dye: 60% Cochineal

131
No mordant
Dye: 30% Cochineal

132
No mordant
Dye: 15% Cochineal

133
Pre-mordant: Chrome
Dye: 60% Cochineal

134
Pre-mordant: Chrome
Dye: 30% Cochineal

135
Pre-mordant: Chrome
Dye: 15% Cochineal

136
One bath – dye with mordant
Mordant: 8% Tin 1
Dye: 40% Cochineal + 5ml Indigo stock, *1-min dip x 1*

137
One bath – dye with mordant
Mordant: 8% Tin 1
Dye: 30% Cochineal + 5ml Indigo stock, *1-min dip x 1*

138
One bath – dye with mordant
Mordant: 8% Tin 1
Dye: 20% Cochineal + 5ml Indigo stock, *1-min dip x 1*

139
One bath – dye with mordant
Mordant: 8% Tin 1
Dye: 40% Cochineal + 5ml Indigo stock, *in-out dip x 2*

140
One bath – dye with mordant
Mordant: 8 % Tin 1
Dye: 30% Cochineal + 5ml Indigo stock, *in-out dip x 2*

141
One bath – dye with mordant
Mordant: 8% Tin 1
Dye: 20% Cochineal + 5ml Indigo stock, *in-out dip x 2*

142
One bath – dye with mordant
Mordant: 8% Tin 1
Dye: 40% Cochineal + 5ml Indigo stock, *in-out dip x 1*

143
One bath – dye with mordant
Mordant: 8% Tin 1
Dye: 30% Cochineal + 5ml Indigo stock, *in-out dip x 1*

144
One bath – dye with mordant
Mordant: 8% Tin 1
Dye: 20% Cochineal + 5ml Indigo stock, *in-out dip x 1*

RECIPES: ALL RECIPES ARE BASED ON THE BASIC MORDANT AND DYE RECIPES IN PART ONE: MORDANTS *SEE* PP.26–7, DYES *SEE* PP.34–5.

ANY VARIATIONS FROM THE BASIC RECIPES, OR STEPS PARTICULAR TO THE INDIVIDUAL RECIPE, ARE WRITTEN IN *ITALICS*.

QUANTITIES: ALL QUANTITIES ARE GIVEN FOR 100G OF YARN (DRY WEIGHT).   WATER PH: ALL RECIPES USE WATER PH 7 (*SEE* P.21).

127 128 129
130 131 132
133 134 135
136 137 138
139 140 141
142 143 144

VIOLET-GREY – GREY-BLACK RECIPES FOR ANIMAL FIBRES

These colours may appear rather dull at first, but they are in fact very effective when used to bring out a particular emphasis of another colour. When the term one bath is used it refers to the method of mordanting whereby the mordant is combined with the dye. Tin is often used this way as the dyestuff tends to reduce the harsh effect of tin on animal fibres. Recipes 151–3 and 154–6 are known as 'one-bath scarlet'.

145
Pre-mordant: Chrome
Dye: 60% Cochineal
After mordant: 1% Iron 1,
simmer for 10 min

146
Pre-mordant: Chrome
Dye: 30% Cochineal
After mordant: 1% Iron 1,
simmer for 10 min

147
Pre-mordant: Chrome
Dye: 15% Cochineal
After mordant: 1% Iron 1,
simmer for 10 min

148
One bath – dye with mordant
Mordant: 2.5% Iron 2
Dye: 60% Cochineal

149
One bath – dye with mordant
Mordant: 2.5% Iron 2
Dye: 30% Cochineal

150
One bath – dye with mordant
Mordant: 2.5% Iron 2
Dye: 15% Cochineal

151
One bath – dye with mordant
Mordant: 8% Tin 1
Dye: 40% Cochineal
After mordant: 1% Iron 1,
simmer for 15 min

152
One bath – dye with mordant
Pre-mordant: 6% Tin 1
Dye: 20% Cochineal
After mordant: 1% Iron 1,
simmer for 15 min

153
One bath – dye with mordant
Mordant: 4% Tin 1
Dye: 10% Cochineal
After mordant: 1% Iron 1,
simmer for 15 min

154
One bath – dye with mordant
Mordant: 8% Tin 1
Dye: 40% Cochineal
After mordant: 1% Iron 1,
simmer for 30 min

155
One bath – dye with mordant
Mordant: 6% Tin 1
Dye: 20% Cochineal
After mordant: 1% Iron 1,
simmer for 30 min

156
One bath – dye with mordant
Mordant: 4% Tin 1
Dye: 10% Cochineal
After mordant: 1% Iron 1,
simmer for 30 min

157
One bath – dye with mordant
Mordant: 2.5% Iron 2,
simmer for 15 min
Dye: 60% Cochineal +
100% Cutch

158
One bath – dye with mordant
Mordant: 2.5% Iron 2,
simmer for 15 min
Dye: 30% Cochineal +
50% Cutch

159
One bath – dye with mordant
Mordant: 2.5% Iron 2,
simmer for 15 min
Dye: 15% Cochineal +
25% Cutch

160
One bath – mordant with dye
Mordant: 6% Tin
Dye: 100% Madder +
60% Cochineal, *do not boil*
Over dye: 5ml Indigo stock,
in-out dip x 2

161
One bath – mordant with dye
Mordant: 6% Tin
Dye: 50% Madder +
30% Cochineal, *do not boil*
Over dye: 5ml Indigo stock,
in-out dip x 2

162
One bath – mordant with dye
Mordant: 6% Tin
Dye: 25% Madder +
15% Cochineal, *do not boil*
Over dye: 5ml Indigo stock,
in-out dip x 2

RECIPES: ALL RECIPES ARE BASED ON THE BASIC MORDANT AND DYE RECIPES IN PART ONE: MORDANTS *SEE* PP.26–7, DYES *SEE* PP.34–5.

ANY VARIATIONS FROM THE BASIC RECIPES, OR STEPS PARTICULAR TO THE INDIVIDUAL RECIPE, ARE WRITTEN IN *ITALICS*.

QUANTITIES: ALL QUANTITIES ARE GIVEN FOR 100G OF YARN (DRY WEIGHT). WATER PH: ALL RECIPES USE WATER PH 7 (*SEE* P.21).

145 146 147
148 149 150
151 152 153
154 155 156
157 158 159
160 161 162

BLUE – VIOLET-BLUE RECIPES FOR ANIMAL FIBRES

It is important to remember to replenish the indigo vat with indigo from the stock solution for darker shades. The longer the dip, the darker the colour. Allow the yarn to fully oxidize before re-dipping, and remember that some depth of shade is lost after rinsing, washing and drying. It is advisable to wait a few days before the final washing with soap.

163
No mordant
Dye: 5ml Indigo stock,
1-min dip x 4

164
No mordant
Dye: 5ml Indigo stock,
1-min dip x 2

165
No mordant
Dye: 5ml Indigo stock,
in-out dip x 1

166
No mordant
Dye: 5ml Indigo stock,
1-min dip x 10

167
No mordant
Dye: 5ml Indigo stock,
1-min dip x 8

168
No mordant
Dye: 5ml Indigo stock,
1-min dip x 6

169
No mordant
Dye: 5ml Indigo stock,
1-min dip x 22

170
No mordant
Dye: 5ml Indigo stock,
1-min dip x 20

171
No mordant
Dye: 5ml Indigo stock,
1-min dip x 18

172
No mordant
Dye: 5ml Indigo stock,
1-min dip x 20
Over dye: 100% Weld,
simmer for 20 min

173
No mordant
Dye: 5ml Indigo stock,
1-min dip x 10
Over dye: 50% Weld,
simmer for 20 min

174
No mordant
Dye: 5ml Indigo stock,
1-min dip x 5
Over dye: 25% Weld,
simmer for 20 min

175
No mordant
Dye: 5ml Indigo stock,
1-min dip x 8
Over dye: 100% Weld,
simmer for 40 min

176
No mordant
Dye: 5ml Indigo stock,
1-min dip x 6
Over dye: 50% Weld,
simmer for 40 min

177
No mordant
Dye: 5ml Indigo stock,
1-min dip x 4
Over dye: 25% Weld,
simmer for 40 min

178
No mordant
Dye: 6% Cochineal
Over dye: 5ml Indigo stock,
1-min dip x 8

179
No mordant
Dye: 3% Cochineal
Over dye: 5ml Indigo stock,
1-min dip x 6

180
No mordant
Dye: 1.5% Cochineal
Over dye: 5ml Indigo stock,
1-min dip x 4

RECIPES: ALL RECIPES ARE BASED ON THE BASIC MORDANT AND DYE RECIPES IN PART ONE: MORDANTS *SEE* PP.26–7, DYES *SEE* PP.34–5. ANY VARIATIONS FROM THE BASIC RECIPES, OR STEPS PARTICULAR TO THE INDIVIDUAL RECIPE, ARE WRITTEN IN *ITALICS*.

QUANTITIES: ALL QUANTITIES ARE GIVEN FOR 100G OF YARN (DRY WEIGHT).   WATER PH: ALL RECIPES USE WATER PH 7 (*SEE* P.21).

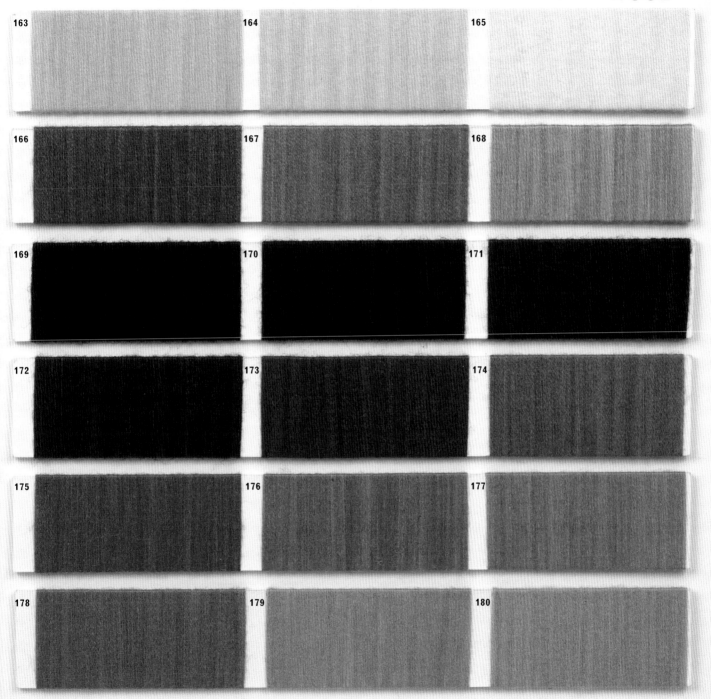

163 164 165
166 167 168
169 170 171
172 173 174
175 176 177
178 179 180

BLUE-GREEN – GREEN-GOLD RECIPES FOR ANIMAL FIBRES

When dyeing with indigo it is difficult to gauge when you have the exact colour you require. This is because the yarn will have to be left to oxidize, rinsed thoroughly and dried before you know what shade you have. The same problem arises with greens, but it is always important to record exactly what you have done and experience over time helps you to gain control.

181
Dye: 5ml Indigo stock,
in-out dip x 10
After mordant: 1% Iron,
simmer for 20 min

182
Dye: 5ml Indigo stock,
in-out dip x 8
After mordant: 1% Iron,
simmer for 20 min

183
Dye: 5ml Indigo stock,
in-out dip x 6
After mordant: 1% Iron,
simmer for 20 min

184
Pre-mordant: Alum
Dye: 25% Weld
Over dye: 5ml Indigo stock,
in-out dip x 7

185
Pre-mordant: Alum
Dye: 25% Weld
Over dye: 5ml Indigo stock,
in-out dip x 6

186
Pre-mordant: Alum
Dye: 25% Weld
Over dye: 5ml Indigo stock,
in-out dip x 4

187
No mordant
Dye: 5ml Indigo stock,
1-min dip x 6
Over dye: 25% Weld,
simmer for 30 min

188
No mordant
Dye: 5ml Indigo stock,
30-sec dip x 4
Over dye: 25% Weld,
simmer for 30 min

189
No mordant
Dye: 5ml Indigo stock,
in-out dip x 2
Over dye: 25% Weld,
simmer for 30 min

190
Pre-mordant: Chrome
Dye: 50% Weld
Over dye: 5ml Indigo stock,
in-out dip x 8

191
Pre-mordant: Chrome
Dye: 50% Weld
Over dye: 5ml Indigo stock,
in-out dip x 6

192
Pre-mordant: Chrome
Dye: 50% Weld
Over dye: 5ml Indigo stock,
in-out dip x 4

193
Pre-mordant: Copper
Dye: 100% Weld

194
Pre-mordant: Copper
Dye: 25% Weld

195
Pre-mordant: Copper
Dye: 12.5% Weld

196
Pre-mordant: Chrome
Dye: 100% Weld
Over dye: 5ml Indigo stock,
in-out dip x 4

197
Pre-mordant: Chrome
Dye: 100% Weld
Over dye: 5ml Indigo stock,
in-out dip x 2

198
Pre-mordant: Chrome
Dye: 100% Weld
Over dye: 5ml Indigo stock,
in-out dip x 1

RECIPES: ALL RECIPES ARE BASED ON THE BASIC MORDANT AND DYE RECIPES IN PART ONE: MORDANTS *SEE* PP.26–7, DYES *SEE* PP.34–5. ANY VARIATIONS FROM THE BASIC RECIPES, OR STEPS PARTICULAR TO THE INDIVIDUAL RECIPE, ARE WRITTEN IN *ITALICS*.

QUANTITIES: ALL QUANTITIES ARE GIVEN FOR 100G OF YARN (DRY WEIGHT).   WATER PH: ALL RECIPES USE WATER PH 7 (*SEE* P.21).

181 182 183
184 185 186
187 188 189
190 191 192
193 194 195
196 197 198

YELLOW-GREEN – GOLD-GREEN RECIPES FOR ANIMAL FIBRES

These colours were created by short dips in the indigo bath to build up the required shade.
Indigo will quickly overpower pale shades if care is not taken.

199
No mordant
Dye: 12.5% Weld
Over dye: 5ml Indigo stock,
in-out dip x 3

200
No mordant
Dye: 12.5% Weld
Over dye: 5ml Indigo stock,
in-out dip x 2

201
No mordant
Dye: 12.5% Weld
Over dye: 5ml Indigo stock,
in-out dip x 1

202
No mordant
Dye: 100% Weld
Over dye: 5ml Indigo stock,
in-out dip x 6

203
No mordant
Dye: 100% Weld
Over dye: 5ml Indigo stock,
in-out dip x 5

204
No mordant
Dye: 100% Weld
Over dye: 5ml Indigo stock,
in-out dip x 4

205
No mordant
Dye: 100% Weld
Over dye: 5ml Indigo stock,
in-out dip x 12

206
No mordant
Dye: 100% Weld
Over dye: 5ml Indigo stock,
in-out dip x 10

207
No mordant
Dye: 100% Weld
Over dye: 5ml Indigo stock,
in-out dip x 8

208
Pre-mordant: Chrome
Dye: 12.5% Weld
Over dye: 5ml Indigo stock,
in-out dip x 3

209
Pre-mordant: Chrome
Dye: 12.5% Weld
Over dye: 5ml Indigo stock,
in-out dip x 2

210
Pre-mordant: Chrome
Dye: 12.5% Weld
Over dye: 5ml Indigo stock,
in-out dip x 1

211
Pre-mordant: Chrome
Dye: 12.5% Weld
Over dye: 5ml Indigo stock,
in-out dip x 6

212
Pre-mordant: Chrome
Dye: 12.5% Weld
Over dye: 5ml Indigo stock,
in-out dip x 5

213
Pre-mordant: Chrome
Dye: 12.5% Weld
Over dye: 5ml Indigo stock,
in-out dip x 4

214
Pre-mordant: Chrome
Dye: 12.5% Weld
Over dye: 5ml Indigo stock,
in-out dip x 10

215
Pre-mordant: Chrome
Dye: 12.5% Weld
Over dye: 5ml Indigo stock,
in-out dip x 9

216
Pre-mordant: Chrome
Dye: 12.5% Weld
Over dye: 5ml Indigo stock,
in-out dip x 8

199 200 201
202 203 204
205 206 207
208 209 210
211 212 213
214 215 216

BLUE-YELLOW – YELLOW-GREEN RECIPES FOR ANIMAL FIBRES

These pale greens have been built up very carefully with short dips until the required colour has been obtained. It is not easy to achieve an even shade with very pale colours and quick dips, and of course the hues will tend to be more sensitive to fading as are most paler shades. However, the colours are so evocative of spring I think they are worth the risk.

217
One bath – mordant with dye
Mordant: 4% Tin 1
Dye: 12.5% Weld
Over dye: 5ml Indigo stock,
in-out dip x 3

218
One bath – mordant with dye
Mordant: 4% Tin 1
Dye: 12.5% Weld
Over dye: 5ml Indigo stock,
in-out dip x 2

219
One bath – mordant with dye
Mordant: 4% Tin 1
Dye: 12.5% Weld
Over dye: 5ml Indigo stock,
in-out dip x 1

220
One bath – mordant with dye
Mordant: 4% Tin 1
Dye: 25% Weld
Over dye: 5ml Indigo stock,
in-out dip x 3

221
One bath – mordant with dye
Mordant: 4% Tin 1
Dye: 25% Weld
Over dye: 5ml Indigo stock,
in-out dip x 2

222
One bath – mordant with dye
Mordant: 4% Tin 1
Dye: 25% Weld
Over dye: 5ml Indigo stock,
in-out dip x 1

223
One bath – mordant with dye
Mordant: 8% Tin 1
Dye: 100% Weld
Over dye: 5ml Indigo stock,
in-out dip x 4

224
One bath – mordant with dye
Mordant: 8% Tin 1
Dye: 100% Weld
Over dye: 5ml Indigo stock,
in-out dip x 2

225
One bath – mordant with dye
Mordant: 8% Tin 1
Dye: 100% Weld
Over dye: 5ml Indigo stock,
in-out dip x 1

226
Pre-mordant: Alum
Dye: 25% Weld
Over dye: 5ml Indigo stock,
30-sec dip x 10

227
Pre-mordant: Alum
Dye: 25% Weld
Over dye: 5ml Indigo stock,
30-sec dip x 6

228
Pre-mordant: Alum
Dye: 25% Weld
Over dye: 5ml Indigo stock,
30-sec dip x 5

229
Pre-mordant: Alum
Dye: 25% Weld
Over dye: 5ml Indigo stock,
in-out dip x 7

230
Pre-mordant: Alum
Dye: 25% Weld
Over dye: 5ml Indigo stock,
in-out dip x 6

231
Pre-mordant: Alum
Dye: 25% Weld
Over dye: 5ml Indigo stock,
in-out dip x 5

232
Pre-mordant: Alum
Dye: 25% Weld
Over dye: 5ml Indigo stock,
in-out dip x 3

233
Pre-mordant: Alum
Dye: 25% Weld
Over dye: 5ml Indigo stock,
in-out dip x 2

234
Pre-mordant: Alum
Dye: 25% Weld
Over dye: 5ml Indigo stock,
in-out dip x 1

RECIPES: ALL RECIPES ARE BASED ON THE BASIC MORDANT AND DYE RECIPES IN PART ONE: MORDANTS *SEE* PP.26–7, DYES *SEE* PP.34–5. ANY VARIATIONS FROM THE BASIC RECIPES, OR STEPS PARTICULAR TO THE INDIVIDUAL RECIPE, ARE WRITTEN IN *ITALICS*.

QUANTITIES: ALL QUANTITIES ARE GIVEN FOR 100G OF YARN (DRY WEIGHT).   WATER PH: ALL RECIPES USE WATER PH 7 (*SEE* P.21).

217
218
219
220
221
222
223
224
225
226
227
228
229
230
231
232
233
234

RED-BROWN – KHAKI-BROWN RECIPES FOR ANIMAL FIBRES

Cutch is one of the few substantive dyes, which means that it has a natural affinity with wool and other animal fibres and does not need a mordant. On its own it yields a warm brown, but this can be extended with the use of mordants and over dyeing. Madder with a chrome mordant and over dyed with indigo gives a cutch-like brown with a slightly warmer tone. The last two cards illustrate how iron can be used to change a colour.

235
Pre-mordant: Chrome
Dye: 100% Cutch

236
Pre-mordant: Chrome
Dye: 50% Cutch

237
Pre-mordant: Chrome
Dye: 25% Cutch

238
No mordant
Dye: 100% Cutch

239
No mordant
Dye: 50% Cutch

240
No mordant
Dye: 25% Cutch

241
Dye: 100% Cutch
After mordant: 1% Iron 1,
simmer for 15 min

242
Dye: 50% Cutch
After mordant: 1% Iron 1,
simmer for 15 min

243
Dye: 25% Cutch
After mordant: 1% Iron 1,
simmer for 15 min

244
Pre-mordant: Chrome
Dye: 100% Madder
Over dye: 5ml Indigo stock,
in-out dip x 1

245
Pre-mordant: Chrome
Dye: 50% Madder
Over dye: 5ml Indigo stock,
in-out dip x 1

246
Pre-mordant: Chrome
Dye: 25% Madder
Over dye: 5ml Indigo stock,
in-out dip x 1

247
Dye: 100% Weld
After mordant: 1% Iron 1,
simmer for 1 min

248
Dye: 25% Weld
After mordant: 1% Iron 1,
simmer for 1 min

249
Dye: 12.5% Weld
After mordant: 1% Iron 1,
simmer for 1 min

250
Dye: 100% Weld
After mordant: 1% Iron 1,
simmer for 15 min

251
Dye: 25% Weld
After mordant: 1% Iron 1,
simmer for 15 min

252
Dye: 12.5% Weld
After mordant: 1% Iron 1,
simmer for 15 min

RECIPES: ALL RECIPES ARE BASED ON THE BASIC MORDANT AND DYE RECIPES IN PART ONE: MORDANTS *SEE* PP.26–7, DYES *SEE* PP.34–5. ANY VARIATIONS FROM THE BASIC RECIPES, OR STEPS PARTICULAR TO THE INDIVIDUAL RECIPE, ARE WRITTEN IN *ITALICS*.

QUANTITIES: ALL QUANTITIES ARE GIVEN FOR 100G OF YARN (DRY WEIGHT).   WATER PH: ALL RECIPES USE WATER PH 7 (*SEE* P.21).

235
236
237
238
239
240
241
242
243
244
245
246
247
248
249
250
251
252

YELLOW RECIPES FOR VEGETABLE FIBRES

These yellows clearly illustrate the difference between the two alum mordant recipes.
Alum 1 gives paler, greener yellows, whereas recipe 2 brings out the warmth in the colour as
well as the deeper, more saturated shades.

1

Tannic acid treatment 1
Pre-mordant: Alum 1
Dye: 25% Weld

2

Tannic acid treatment 1
Pre-mordant: Alum 1
Dye: 12.5% Weld

3

Tannic acid treatment 1
Pre-mordant: Alum 1
Dye: 6.25% Weld

4

Tannic acid treatment 1
Pre-mordant: Alum 1
Dye: 400% Weld

5

Tannic acid treatment 1
Pre-mordant: Alum 1
Dye: 100% Weld

6

Tannic acid treatment 1
Pre-mordant: Alum 1
Dye: 50% Weld

7

Tannic acid treatment 1
Pre-mordant 1: Alum 1
Pre-mordant 2: Copper
Dye: 100% Weld

8

Tannic acid treatment 1
Pre-mordant 1: Alum 1
Pre-mordant 2: Copper
Dye: 50% Weld

9

Tannic acid treatment 1
Pre-mordant 1: Alum 1
Pre-mordant 2: Copper
Dye: 25% Weld

10

Tannic acid treatment 1
Pre-mordant: Alum 2
Dye: 300% Weld

11

Tannic acid treatment 2
Pre-mordant: Alum 2
Dye: 150% Weld

12

Tannic acid treatment 2
Pre-mordant: Alum 2
Dye: 75% Weld

13

Oil treatment
Tannic acid treatment 2
Pre-mordant: Alum 2
Dye: 200% Weld,
no soaping process

14

Oil treatment
Tannic acid treatment 2
Pre-mordant: Alum 2
Dye: 75% Weld,
no soaping process

15

Oil treatment
Tannic acid treatment 2
Pre-mordant: Alum 2
Dye: 25% Weld,
no soaping process

16

Oil treatment
Tannic acid treatment 2
Pre-mordant: Alum 2
Dye: 200% Weld, *soaping process
as in Madder 2*

17

Oil treatment
Tannic acid treatment 2
Pre-mordant: Alum 2
Dye: 75% Weld, *soaping process
as in Madder 2*

18

Oil treatment
Tannic acid treatment 2
Pre-mordant: Alum 2
Dye: 25% Weld, *soaping process
as in Madder 2*

RECIPES: ALL RECIPES ARE BASED ON THE BASIC TREATMENT, MORDANT AND DYE RECIPES IN PART ONE: TREATMENTS AND MORDANTS *SEE* PP.28–9,
DYES *SEE* PP.37–8. ANY VARIATIONS FROM THE BASIC RECIPES, OR STEPS PARTICULAR TO THE INDIVIDUAL RECIPES, ARE WRITTEN IN *ITALICS*.
QUANTITIES: ALL QUANTITIES ARE GIVEN FOR 100G OF YARN (DRY WEIGHT). **WATER PH:** ALL RECIPES USE WATER PH 7 (*SEE* P.21).

One-bath chrome, in which the mordant is combined with dye in the same dye bath, gives a much paler shade (21) than colours based on pre-mordanted chrome (shades 19–20). The shades using the oil treatment give a denser shade and mask the natural lustre of the yarn, but the colours are interesting enough to make this worthwhile.

19
Tannic acid treatment 1
Pre-mordant: Chrome
Dye: 50% Weld

20
Tannic acid treatment 1
Pre-mordant: Chrome
Dye: 25% Weld

21
Tannic acid treatment 1
One bath – dye with mordant
Mordant: Chrome
Dye: 12.5% Weld

22
Tannic acid treatment 1
Pre-mordant: Alum 1
Dye: 200% Weld + 2% Cutch

23
Tannic acid treatment 1
Pre-mordant: Alum 1
Dye: 100% Weld + 1% Cutch

24
Tannic acid treatment 1
Pre-mordant: Alum 1
Dye: 50% Weld + 0.5% Cutch

25
Oil treatment
Tannic acid treatment 2
Pre-mordant: Alum 2
Dye: 400% Weld + 3% Cochineal
Over dye: 100% Weld, *soaping process as in Madder 2*

26
Oil treatment
Tannic acid treatment 2
Pre-mordant: Alum 2
Dye: 200% Weld + 2% Cochineal
Over dye: 100% Weld, *soaping process as in Madder 2*

27
Oil treatment
Tannic acid treatment 2
Pre-mordant: Alum 2
Dye: 75% Weld + 1% Cochineal
Over dye: 100% Weld, *soaping process as in Madder 2*

28
Oil treatment
Tannic acid treatment 2
Pre-mordant: Alum 2
Dye: 150% Madder 2
Over dye: 200% Weld

29
Oil treatment
Tannic acid treatment 2
Pre-mordant: Alum 2
Dye: 75% Madder 2
Over dye: 200% Weld

30
Oil treatment
Tannic acid treatment 2
Pre-mordant: Alum 2
Dye: 37.5% Madder 2
Over dye: 200% Weld

31
Oil treatment
Tannic acid treatment 2
Pre-mordant: Alum 2
Dye: 200% Weld
Over dye: 2% Cochineal, *soaping process as in Madder 2*

32
Oil treatment
Tannic acid treatment 2
Pre-mordant: Alum 2
Dye: 100% Weld
Over dye: 1% Cochineal, *soaping process as in Madder 2*

33
Oil treatment
Tannic acid treatment 2
Pre-mordant: Alum 2
Dye: 75% Weld
Over dye: 0.5% Cochineal, *soaping process as in Madder 2*

34
Tannic acid treatment 1
Pre-mordant: Alum 1
Dye: 200% Madder 1 + 200% Weld, *do not boil*

35
Tannic acid treatment 1
Pre-mordant: Alum 1
Dye: 100% Madder 1 + 100% Weld, *do not boil*

36
Tannic acid treatment 1
Pre-mordant: Alum 1
Dye: 50% Madder 1 + 50% Weld, *do not boil*

RECIPES: ALL RECIPES ARE BASED ON THE BASIC TREATMENT, MORDANT AND DYE RECIPES IN PART ONE: TREATMENTS AND MORDANTS *SEE* PP.28–9, DYES *SEE* PP.37–8. ANY VARIATIONS FROM THE BASIC RECIPES, OR STEPS PARTICULAR TO THE INDIVIDUAL RECIPES, ARE WRITTEN IN *ITALICS*.

QUANTITIES: ALL QUANTITIES ARE GIVEN FOR 100G OF YARN (DRY WEIGHT). **WATER PH:** ALL RECIPES USE WATER PH 7 (*SEE* P.21).

PINK – RED RECIPES FOR VEGETABLE FIBRES

Madder treated with Turkey red oil produces the colour Turkey red (shades 43–51). Tin used in a one-bath method as used for animal fibres seems to act as a resist against the dye forming an insoluble tin soap, which results in pale flesh colours, quite different from colours achieved with the animal fibres. Tin is most effective as a modifier in the soaping process of clearing to give more brilliancy to the colour.

37
Tannic acid treatment 1
One bath – dye with mordant
Mordant: Tin
Dye: 100% Madder 1

38
Tannic acid treatment 1
One bath – dye with mordant
Mordant: Tin
Dye: 50% Madder 1

39
Tannic acid treatment 1
One bath – dye with mordant
Mordant: Tin
Dye: 25% Madder 1

40
Tannic Acid Treatment 2
Pre-mordant: Alum 2
Dye: 25% Madder 1

41
Tannic acid treatment 2
Pre-mordant: Alum 2
Dye: 12.5% Madder 1

42
Tannic acid treatment 2
Pre-mordant: Alum 2
Dye: 6.25% Madder 1

43
Oil treatment
Tannic acid treatment 2
Pre-mordant: Alum 2
Dye: 150% Madder 2,
no soaping process

44
Oil treatment
Tannic Acid Treatment 2
Pre-mordant: Alum 2
Dye: 75% Madder 2,
no soaping process

45
Oil treatment
Tannic acid treatment 2
Pre-mordant: Alum 2
Dye: 37.5% Madder 2,
no soaping process

46
Oil treatment
Tannic acid treatment 2
Pre-mordant: Alum 2
Dye: 200% Madder 2,
soaped with 1% Tin

47
Oil treatment
Tannic acid treatment 2
Pre-mordant: Alum 2
Dye: 100% Madder 2,
soaped with 1% Tin

48
Oil treatment
Tannic acid treatment 2
Pre-mordant: Alum 2
Dye: 50% Madder 2,
soaped with 1% Tin

49
Oil treatment
Tannic acid treatment 2
Pre-mordant: Alum 2
Dye: 100% Madder 2

50
Oil treatment
Tannic acid treatment 2
Pre-mordant: Alum 2
Dye: 50% Madder 2

51
Oil treatment
Tannic acid treatment 2
Pre-mordant: Alum 2
Dye: 25% Madder 2

52
Tannic acid treatment 1
Pre-mordant: Alum 1
Dye: 200% Madder 1, *step 5:
re-heat for 20 min*

53
Tannic acid treatment 1
Pre-mordant: Alum 1
Dye: 100% Madder 1, *step 5:
re-heat for 20 min*

54
Tannic acid treatment 1
Pre-mordant: Alum 1
Dye: 50% Madder 1, *step 5:
re-heat for 20 min*

RECIPES: ALL RECIPES ARE BASED ON THE BASIC TREATMENT, MORDANT AND DYE RECIPES IN PART ONE: TREATMENTS AND MORDANTS *SEE* PP.28–9, DYES *SEE* PP.37–8. ANY VARIATIONS FROM THE BASIC RECIPES, OR STEPS PARTICULAR TO THE INDIVIDUAL RECIPES, ARE WRITTEN IN *ITALICS*.

QUANTITIES: ALL QUANTITIES ARE GIVEN FOR 100G OF YARN (DRY WEIGHT). WATER PH: ALL RECIPES USE WATER PH 7 (*SEE* P.21).

37

38

39

40

41

42

43

44

45

46

47

48

49

50

51

52

53

54

PINK – MAGENTA – CERISE RECIPES FOR VEGETABLE FIBRES

I used oil with cochineal, with good results. Traditionally oil is only used with madder to produce Turkey red. This treatment allows much richer shades to be obtained, but does flatten the natural lustre of the yarn, and gives it the oily odour for which Turkey red is so famous. It takes a long time to get a colour, but the results are intense and lively. The key to success is in the steaming.

55
Oil treatment
Tannic acid treatment 2
Pre-mordant: Alum 2
Dye: 12.5% Cochineal, *soaping process as in Madder 2*

56
Oil treatment
Tannic acid treatment 2
Pre-mordant: Alum 2
Dye: 6.25% Cochineal, *soaping process as in Madder 2*

57
Oil treatment
Tannic acid treatment 2
Pre-mordant: Alum 2
Dye: 3% Cochineal, *soaping process as in Madder 2*

58
Oil treatment
Tannic acid treatment 2
Pre-mordant: Alum 2
Dye: 12.5% Cochineal, *no soaping process*

59
Oil treatment
Tannic acid treatment 2
Pre-mordant: Alum 2

Dye: 6.25% Cochineal, *no soaping process*

60
Oil treatment
Tannic acid treatment 2
Pre-mordant: Alum 2
Dye: 3% Cochineal, *no soaping process*

61
Oil treatment
Tannic acid treatment 2
Pre-mordant: Alum 2
Dye: 100% Cochineal, *soaping process as in Madder 2*

62
Oil treatment
Tannic acid treatment 2
Pre-mordant: Alum 2
Dye: 50% Cochineal, *soaping process as in Madder 2*

63
Oil treatment
Tannic acid treatment 2
Pre-mordant: Alum 2
Dye: 25% Cochineal, *soaping process as in Madder 2*

64
Oil treatment
Tannic acid treatment 2
Pre-mordant: Alum 2
Dye: 150% Madder 2 + 100% Cochineal exhaust, *do not boil; no soaping process*

65
Oil treatment
Tannic acid treatment 2
Pre-mordant: Alum 2
Dye: 75% Madder 2 + 50% Cochineal exhaust, *do not boil; no soaping process*

66
Oil treatment
Tannic acid treatment 2
Pre-mordant: Alum 2
Dye: 50% Madder 2 + 25% Cochineal, *do not boil; no soaping process*

67
Oil treatment
Tannic acid treatment 2
Pre-mordant: Alum 2
Dye: 150% Madder 2 + 100% Cochineal, *do not boil*

68
Oil treatment
Tannic acid treatment 2
Pre-mordant: Alum 2
Dye: 75% Madder 2 + 50% Cochineal, *do not boil*

69
Oil treatment
Tannic acid treatment 2
Pre-mordant: Alum 2
Dye: 50% Madder 2 + 25% Cochineal, *do not boil*

70
Oil treatment
Tannic acid treatment 2
Pre-mordant: Alum 2
Dye: 500% Madder 2

71
Oil treatment
Tannic acid treatment 2
Pre-mordant: Alum 2
Dye: 300% Madder 2

72
Oil treatment
Tannic acid treatment 2
Pre-mordant: Alum 2
Dye: 200% Madder 2

RECIPES: ALL RECIPES ARE BASED ON THE BASIC TREATMENT, MORDANT AND DYE RECIPES IN PART ONE: TREATMENTS AND MORDANTS *SEE* PP.28–9, DYES *SEE* PP.37–8. ANY VARIATIONS FROM THE BASIC RECIPES, OR STEPS PARTICULAR TO THE INDIVIDUAL RECIPES, ARE WRITTEN IN *ITALICS*.

QUANTITIES: ALL QUANTITIES ARE GIVEN FOR 100G OF YARN (DRY WEIGHT). WATER PH: ALL RECIPES USE WATER PH 7 (*SEE* P.21).

PINK – BROWN RECIPES FOR VEGETABLE FIBRES

The last card shows chrome mordanted separately and then dyed in madder – this yields a much stronger shade than the one-bath method (shade 76). The first alum recipe yields paler shades than the second. The pale pinks are soft and rose like.

73

Tannic acid treatment 2
Pre-mordant: Alum 2
Dye: 100% Cochineal

74

Tannic acid treatment 2
Pre-mordant: Alum 2
Dye: 50% Cochineal

75

Tannic acid treatment 2
Pre-mordant: Alum 2
Dye: 25% Cochineal

76

Tannic acid treatment 1
One bath – dye with mordant
Mordant: Chrome
Dye: 50% Madder 1

77

Tannic acid treatment 1
One bath – dye with mordant
Mordant: Chrome
Dye: 25% Madder 1

78

Tannic acid treatment 1
One bath – dye with mordant
Mordant: Chrome
Dye: 12.5% Madder 1

79

Tannic acid treatment 1
One bath – dye with mordant
Mordant: Chrome
Dye: 400% Madder 1

80

Tannic acid treatment 1
One bath – dye with mordant
Mordant: Chrome
Dye: 200% Madder 1

81

Tannic acid treatment 1
One bath – dye with mordant
Mordant: Chrome
Dye: 100% Madder 1

82

Tannic acid treatment 1
Pre-mordant: Alum 1
Dye: 100% Madder 1
After mordant: 0.5% Iron

83

Tannic acid treatment 1
Pre-mordant: Alum 1
Dye: 50% Madder 1
After mordant: 0.5% Iron

84

Tannic acid treatment 1
Pre-mordant: Alum 1
Dye: 25% Madder 1
After mordant: 0.5% Iron

85

Tannic acid treatment 1
Pre-mordant 1: Alum 1
Pre-mordant 2: Copper
Dye: 100% Madder 1

86

Tannic acid treatment 1
Pre-mordant 1: Alum 1
Pre-mordant 2: Copper
Dye: 50% Madder 1

87

Tannic acid treatment 1
Pre-mordant 1: Alum 1
Pre-mordant 2: Copper
Dye: 25% Madder 1

88

Tannic acid treatment 1
Pre-mordant: Chrome
Dye: 100% Madder 1

89

Tannic acid treatment 1
Pre-mordant: Chrome
Dye: 50% Madder 1

90

Tannic acid treatment 1
Pre-mordant: Chrome
Dye: 25% Madder 1

RECIPES: ALL RECIPES ARE BASED ON THE BASIC TREATMENT, MORDANT AND DYE RECIPES IN PART ONE: TREATMENTS AND MORDANTS *SEE* PP.28–9, DYES *SEE* PP.37–8. ANY VARIATIONS FROM THE BASIC RECIPES, OR STEPS PARTICULAR TO THE INDIVIDUAL RECIPES, ARE WRITTEN IN *ITALICS*.

QUANTITIES: ALL QUANTITIES ARE GIVEN FOR 100G OF YARN (DRY WEIGHT).   **WATER PH:** ALL RECIPES USE WATER PH 7 (*SEE* P.21).

73 74 75
76 77 78
79 80 81
82 83 84
85 86 87
88 89 90

PINK – BURGUNDY RECIPES FOR VEGETABLE FIBRES

I experimented with multiple mordanting to see what effects I could achieve. Though the colours are attractive, similar shades can be achieved more easily using alum recipe 2 (shades 73–5). Recipes using tannic acid treatment 2 and alum 2 yield deeper shades than those using tannic acid treatment 1 and alum 1.

91
Tannic acid treatment 1
Pre-mordant 1: Alum 1
Pre-mordant 2: Copper
One bath – dye with mordant
Mordant: Tin
Dye: 100% Cochineal

92
Tannic acid treatment 1
Pre-mordant 1: Alum 1
Pre-mordant 2: Copper
One bath – dye with mordant
Mordant: Tin
Dye: 50% Cochineal

93
Tannic acid treatment 1
Pre-mordant 1: Alum 1
Pre-mordant 2: Copper
One bath – dye with mordant
Mordant: Tin
Dye: 25% Cochineal

94
Tannic acid treatment 1
Pre-mordant: Copper
Dye: 200% Madder 1 + 100% Cochineal, *do not boil; soak for 4 days, re-heat, rinse and dry*

95
Tannic acid treatment 1
Pre-mordant: Copper
Dye: 100% Madder 1 + 50% Cochineal, *do not boil; soak for 4 days, re-heat, rinse and dry*

96
Tannic acid treatment 1
Pre-mordant: Copper
Dye: 50% Madder 1 + 25% Cochineal, *do not boil; soak for 4 days, re-heat, rinse and dry*

97
Tannic acid treatment 1
Pre-mordant: Alum 1
Dye: 400% Madder 1
Over dye: 0.25g Indigo, *in-out dips x 4*

98
Tannic acid treatment 1
Pre-mordant: Alum 1
Dye: 400% Madder 1
Over dye: 0.25g Indigo, *in-out dip x 2*

99
Tannic acid treatment 1
Pre-mordant: Alum 1
Dye: 400% Madder 1
Over dye: 0.25g Indigo, *in-out dip x 4*

100
Tannic acid treatment 1
Pre-mordant: Alum 1
Dye: 100% Madder 1
Over dye: 0.25g Indigo, *in-out dip x 4*

101
Tannic acid treatment 1
Pre-mordant: Alum 1
Dye: 100% Madder 1
Over dye: 0.25g Indigo, *in-out dip x 2*

102
Tannic acid treatment 1
Pre-mordant: Alum 1
Dye: 100% Madder 1
Over dye: 0.25g Indigo, *in-out dip x 1*

103
Tannic acid treatment 2
Pre-mordant: Chrome
Dye: 400% Madder 1

104
Tannic acid treatment 2
Pre-mordant: Chrome
Dye: 300% Madder 1

105
Tannic acid treatment 2
Pre-mordant: Chrome
Dye: 200% Madder 1

106
Tannic acid treatment 2
Pre-mordant: Alum 2
Dye: 75% Madder 1
Over dye: 0.4g Indigo, *5-min dip x 1*

107
Tannic acid treatment
Pre-mordant: Alum 2
Dye: 75% Madder 1
Over dye: 0.25g Indigo, *5-min dip x 1*

108
Tannic acid treatment 2
Pre-mordant: Alum 2
Dye: 75% Madder 1
Over dye: 0.25g Indigo, *in-out dip x 1*

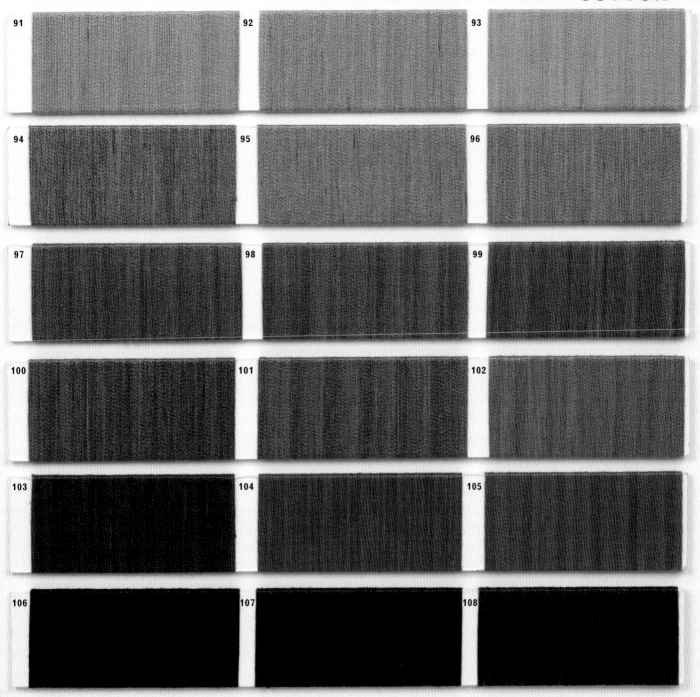

91
92
93
94
95
96
97
98
99
100
101
102
103
104
105
106
107
108

VIOLET – DEEP RED-VIOLET RECIPES FOR VEGETABLE FIBRES

Many more subtle variations of violet could be achieved with careful experimentation with over dyeing. The evenness of the indigo was difficult to control, but I still liked the results.

109
Tannic acid treatment 1
Pre-mordant 1: Alum 1
Pre-mordant 2: Copper
Dye: 100% Cochineal

110
Tannic acid treatment 1
Pre-mordant 1: Alum 1
Pre-mordant 2: Copper
Dye: 50% Cochineal

111
Tannic acid treatment 1
Pre-mordant 1: Alum 1
Pre-mordant 2: Copper
Dye: 25% Cochineal

112
Tannic acid treatment 1
Pre-mordant: Alum 1
Dye: 25% Madder 1
Over dye: 0.25g Indigo,
in-out dip x 4

113
Tannic acid treatment 1
Pre-mordant: Alum 1
Dye: 25% Madder 1
Over dye: 0.25g Indigo,
in-out dip x 2

114
Tannic acid treatment 1
Pre-mordant: Alum 1
Dye 1: 25% Madder 1
Over dye 2: 0.25g Indigo,
in-out dip x 1

115
Oil treatment
Tannic acid treatment 2
Pre-mordant: Alum 2
Dye: 12.5% Cochineal
Over dye 2: 0.25g Indigo,
1-min dip x 1

116
Oil treatment
Tannic acid treatment 2
Pre-mordant: Alum 2
Dye: 6.25% Cochineal
Over dye: 0.25g Indigo,
1-min dip x 1

117
Oil treatment
Tannic acid treatment 2
Pre-mordant: Alum 2
Dye: 3% Cochineal
Over dye: 0.25g Indigo,
1-min dip x 1

118
Oil treatment
Tannic acid treatment 2
Pre-mordant: Alum 2
Dye: 100% Cochineal
Over dye: 1g Indigo, *5-min dip x 1*

119
Oil treatment
Tannic acid treatment 2
Pre-mordant: Alum 2
Dye: 50% Cochineal
Over dye: 1g Indigo, *5-min dip x 1*

120
Oil treatment
Tannic acid treatment 2
Pre-mordant: Alum 2
Dye: 25% Cochineal
Over dye: 1g Indigo, *5-min dip x 1*

121
Oil treatment
Tannic acid treatment 2
Pre-mordant: Alum 2
Dye: 200% Madder 2
Over dye: 0.5g Indigo, *5-min dip x 2*

122
Oil treatment
Tannic acid treatment 2
Pre-mordant: Alum 2
Dye: 100% Madder 2
Over dye: 0.5g Indigo, *1-min dip x 1*

123
Oil treatment
Tannic acid treatment 2
Pre-mordant: Alum 2
Dye: 50% Madder 2
Over dye: 0.5g Indigo,
in-out dip x 1

124
Tannic acid treatment 2
Pre-mordant: Chrome
Dye: 400% Madder 1
Over dye 1: 75% Cochineal
Over dye 2: 150% Madder 1
1st exhaust
Over dye 3: 0.5g Indigo,
1-min dip x 4

125
Tannic acid treatment 2
Pre-mordant: Chrome
Dye: 300% Madder 1
Over dye 1: 50% Cochineal
Over dye 2: 0.5g Indigo,
1-min dip x 2

126
Tannic acid treatment 2
Pre-mordant: Chrome
Dye: 200% Madder 1
Over dye 1: 25% Cochineal
Over dye 2: 0.5g Indigo,
1-min dip x 1

RECIPES: ALL RECIPES ARE BASED ON THE BASIC TREATMENT, MORDANT AND DYE RECIPES IN PART ONE: TREATMENTS AND MORDANTS *SEE* PP.28–9,
DYES *SEE* PP.37–8. ANY VARIATIONS FROM THE BASIC RECIPES, OR STEPS PARTICULAR TO THE INDIVIDUAL RECIPES, ARE WRITTEN IN *ITALICS*.
QUANTITIES: ALL QUANTITIES ARE GIVEN FOR 100G OF YARN (DRY WEIGHT).   **WATER PH:** ALL RECIPES USE WATER PH 7 (*SEE* P.21).

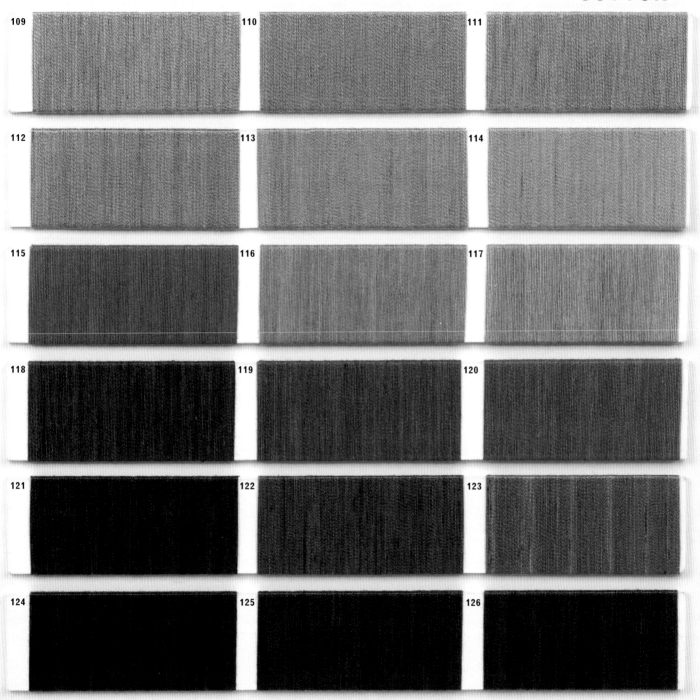

BLUE RECIPES FOR VEGETABLE FIBRES

The variety of blues illustrated here is simply down to the concentration of indigo used and the number of dips. Where tannic acid is used before indigo, the pale blues have a golden under glow.

127
No mordant
Dye: 0.25g Indigo,
1-min dip x 2

128
No mordant
Dye: 0.25g Indigo,
1-min dip x 1

129
No mordant
Dye: 0.25g Indigo,
in-out dip x 1

130
Tannic acid treatment 1
Pre-mordant: Alum 1
Dye: 0.25g Indigo,
1-min dip x 2

131
Tannic acid treatment 1
Pre-mordant: Alum 1
Dye: 0.25g Indigo,
1-min dip x 1

132
Tannic acid treatment 1
Pre-mordant: Alum 1
Dye: 0.25g Indigo,
in-out dip x 1

133
No mordant
Dye: 0.5g Indigo,
2-min dip x 6

134
No mordant
Dye: 0.5g Indigo,
2-min dip x 4

135
No mordant
Dye: 0.5g Indigo,
2-min dip x 2

136
No mordant
Dye: 1g Indigo,
1-min dip x 6

137
No mordant
Dye: 1g Indigo,
1-min dip x 4

138
No mordant
Dye: 1g Indigo,
1-min dip x 2

139
No mordant
Dye: 1g Indigo,
15-min dip x 4

140
No mordant
Dye: 1g Indigo,
15-min dip x 3

141
No mordant
Dye: 1g Indigo,
15-min dip x 2

142
No mordant
Dye: 1g Indigo,
15-min dip x 7

143
No mordant
Dye: 1g Indigo,
15-min dip x 6

144
No mordant
Dye: 1g Indigo,
15-min dip x 5

RECIPES: ALL RECIPES ARE BASED ON THE BASIC TREATMENT, MORDANT AND DYE RECIPES IN PART ONE: TREATMENTS AND MORDANTS *SEE* PP.28–9, DYES *SEE* PP.37–8. ANY VARIATIONS FROM THE BASIC RECIPES, OR STEPS PARTICULAR TO THE INDIVIDUAL RECIPES, ARE WRITTEN IN *ITALICS*.

QUANTITIES: ALL QUANTITIES ARE GIVEN FOR 100G OF YARN (DRY WEIGHT). **WATER PH:** ALL RECIPES USE WATER PH 7 (*SEE* P.21).

127 128 129
130 131 132
133 134 135
136 137 138
139 140 141
142 143 144

DARK BLUE – GREEN-BLUE RECIPES FOR VEGETABLE FIBRES

It is possible to extend the range of blues by adding weld to make the blue greener or cutch to darken and add a brownish tinge. Iron also has a darkening effect though it is much subtler than cutch.

145
No mordant
Dye: 0.5g Indigo,
1-min dip x 6
Over dye: 100% Weld,
simmer for 20 min

146
No mordant
Dye: 0.5g Indigo,
1-min dip x 4
Over dye: 100% Weld,
simmer for 20 min

147
No mordant
Dye: 0.5g Indigo,
1-min dip x 2
Over dye: 100% Weld,
simmer for 20 min

148
No mordant
Tannic acid treatment 2
Dye: 0.5g Indigo,
1-min dip x 4

149
No mordant
Tannic acid treatment 2
Dye: 0.5g Indigo,
1-min dip x 2

150
No mordant
Tannic acid treatment 2
Dye: 0.5g Indigo,
1-min dip x 1

151
No mordant
Dye: 1g Indigo,
1-min dip x 4
Dye: 25% Weld

152
No mordant
Dye: 1g Indigo,
1-min dip x 3
Over dye: 12.5% Weld

153
No mordant
Dye: 1g Indigo,
1-min dip x 1
Over dye: 6.25% Weld

154
Dye: 4g Indigo,
1-min dip x 4
Over dye: 50% Weld
After mordant: 2% Iron

155
Dye: 4g Indigo,
1-min dip x 3
Over dye: 50% Weld
After mordant: 2% Iron

156
Dye: 4g Indigo,
1-min dip x 2
Over dye: 50% Weld
After mordant: 2% Iron

157
Dye: 3g Indigo,
2-min dip x 4
After mordant: 2% Iron
Over dye 1: 3g Indigo,
2-min dip x 4
Over dye 2: 20% Cutch

158
Dye: 3g Indigo,
2-min dip x 2
After mordant: 2% Iron
Over dye 1: 3g Indigo,
2-min dip x 2
Over dye 2: 10% Cutch

159
Dye: 3g Indigo,
2-min dip x 1
After mordant: 2% Iron
Over dye 1: 3g Indigo,
2-min dip x 1
Over dye 2: 5% Cutch

160
No mordant
Dye: 20% Cutch
Over dye 1: 3g Indigo,
10-min dip x 5
Over dye 2: 10% Cutch

161
No mordant
Dye: 10% Cutch
Over dye 1: 3g Indigo vat,
10-min dip x 4
Over dye 2: 10% Cutch

162
No mordant
Dye: 20% Cutch
Over dye 1: 3g Indigo,
2-min dip x 3
Over dye 2: 10% Cutch

RECIPES: ALL RECIPES ARE BASED ON THE BASIC TREATMENT, MORDANT AND DYE RECIPES IN PART ONE: TREATMENTS AND MORDANTS *SEE* PP.28–9,
DYES *SEE* PP.37–8. ANY VARIATIONS FROM THE BASIC RECIPES, OR STEPS PARTICULAR TO THE INDIVIDUAL RECIPES, ARE WRITTEN IN *ITALICS*.
QUANTITIES: ALL QUANTITIES ARE GIVEN FOR 100G OF YARN (DRY WEIGHT). **WATER PH:** ALL RECIPES USE WATER PH 7 (*SEE* P.21).

145 146 147
148 149 150
151 152 153
154 155 156
157 158 159
160 161 162

BLUE-GREEN RECIPES FOR VEGETABLE FIBRES

All these shades have been over dyed either with weld over indigo or indigo over weld. The over dyeing is used to shift the emphasis of the colour from blue to greenish blue or yellow to green.

163
No mordant
Tannic acid treatment 2
Dye: 0.25g Indigo, *1-min dip x 2*
Over dye: 6.25% Weld

164
No mordant
Tannic acid treatment 2
Dye: 0.25g Indigo, *1-min dip x 2*
Over dye: 12.5% Weld

165
No mordant
Tannic acid treatment 2
Dye: 0.25g Indigo, *1-min dip x 2*
Over dye: 25% Weld

166
No mordant
Tannic acid treatment 2
Dye: 0.25g Indigo, *1-min dip x 2*
Over dye: 100% Weld,
simmer for 1 hr

167
No mordant
Tannic acid treatment 2
Dye: 0.25g Indigo, *1-min dip x 2*
Dye: 50% Weld,
simmer for 1 hr

168
No mordant
Tannic acid treatment 2
Dye: 0.25g Indigo, *1-min dip x 2*
Over dye: 25% Weld,
simmer for 1 hr

169
Tannic acid treatment 2
Pre-mordant: Alum 2
Dye: 25% Weld
Over dye: 0.25g Indigo,
1-min dip x 2

170
Tannic acid treatment 2
Pre-mordant: Alum 2
Dye: 25% Weld
Over dye: 0.25g Indigo,
1-min dip x 1

171
Tannic acid treatment 2
Pre-mordant: Alum 2
Dye: 25% Weld
Over dye: 0.25g Indigo,
in-out dip x 1

172
No mordant
Tannic acid treatment 2
Dye: 0.25g Indigo, *1-min dip x 4*
Over dye: 6.25% Weld,
simmer for 20 min

173
No mordant
Tannic acid treatment 2
Dye: 0.25g Indigo, *1-min dip x 4*
Over dye: 12.5% Weld,
simmer for 20 min

174
No mordant
Tannic acid treatment 2
Dye: 0.25g Indigo, *1-min dip x 4*
Over dye: 25% Weld,
simmer for 20 min

175
No mordant
Tannic acid treatment 2
Dye: 0.25g Indigo, *1-min dip x 4*
Over dye: 50% Weld,
simmer for 1 hr

176
No mordant
Tannic acid treatment 2
Dye: 0.25g Indigo, *1-min dip x 2*
Over dye: 25% Weld,
simmer for 1 hr

177
No mordant
Tannic acid treatment 2
Dye: 0.25g Indigo, *1-min dip x 1*
Over dye: 12.5% Weld,
simmer for 1 hr

178
No mordant
Tannic acid treatment 2
Dye: 0.25g Indigo, *1-min dip x 4*
Over dye 1: 6.25% Weld,
simmer for 20 min
Over dye 2: 500% Weld

179
No mordant
Tannic acid treatment 2
Dye: 0.25g Indigo, *1-min dip x 4*
Over dye 1: 6.25% Weld,
simmer for 20 min
Over dye 2: 400% Weld

180
No mordant
Tannic acid treatment 2
Dye: 0.25g Indigo, *1-min dip x 4*
Over dye 1: 6.25% Weld,
simmer for 20 min
Over dye 2: 300% Weld

RECIPES: ALL RECIPES ARE BASED ON THE BASIC TREATMENT, MORDANT AND DYE RECIPES IN PART ONE: TREATMENTS AND MORDANTS *SEE* PP.28–9, DYES *SEE* PP.37–8. ANY VARIATIONS FROM THE BASIC RECIPES, OR STEPS PARTICULAR TO THE INDIVIDUAL RECIPES, ARE WRITTEN IN *ITALICS*.

QUANTITIES: ALL QUANTITIES ARE GIVEN FOR 100G OF YARN (DRY WEIGHT).   **WATER PH:** ALL RECIPES USE WATER PH 7 (*SEE* P.21).

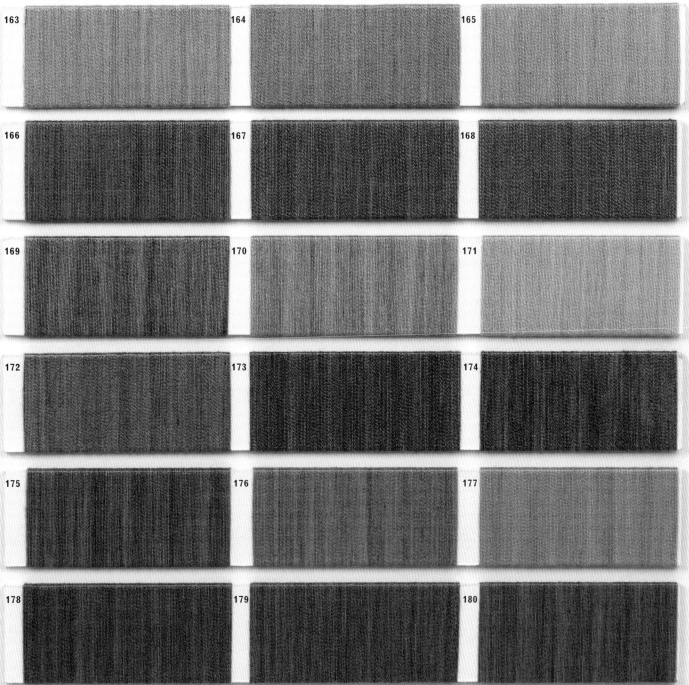

163
164
165
166
167
168
169
170
171
172
173
174
175
176
177
178
179
180

YELLOW-GREEN – DARK GREEN RECIPES FOR VEGETABLE FIBRES

This set of greens indicates the range it is possible to achieve from the yellow end of the spectrum through to the blue again. Control of evenness is more difficult with the paler shades.

181
Tannic acid treatment 2
Pre-mordant: Alum 2
Dye: 75% Weld
Over dye: 0.25g Indigo,
1-min dip x 2

182
Tannic acid treatment 2
Pre-mordant: Alum 2
Dye: 75% Weld
Over dye: 0.25g Indigo,
1-min dip x 1

183
Tannic acid treatment 2
Pre-mordant: Alum 2
Dye: 75% Weld
Over dye: 0.25g Indigo,
in-out dip x 1

184
Tannic acid treatment 2
Pre-mordant: Alum 2
Dye: 25% Weld
Over dye: 0.25g Indigo,
5-min dip x 6

185
Tannic acid treatment 2
Pre-mordant: Alum 2
Dye: 25% Weld
Over dye: 0.25g Indigo,
5-min dip x 4

186
Tannic acid treatment 2
Pre-mordant: Alum 2
Dye: 25% Weld
Over dye: 0.25g Indigo,
in-out dip x 1

187
Tannic acid treatment 2
Pre-mordant: Chrome
Dye: 25% Weld
Over dye: 0.25g Indigo,
5-min dip x 6

188
Tannic acid treatment 2
Pre-mordant: Chrome
Dye: 25% Weld
Over dye: 0.25g Indigo,
5-min dip x 4

189
Tannic acid treatment 2
Pre-mordant: Chrome
Dye: 25% Weld
Over dye: 0.25g Indigo,
in-out dip x 1

190
Tannic acid treatment 2
Pre-mordant: Alum 2
Dye: 300% Weld
Over dye: 0.3g Indigo,
15-min dip x 3

191
Tannic acid treatment 2
Pre-mordant: Alum 2
Dye: 300% Weld
Over dye: 0.3g Indigo,
15-min dip x 2

192
Tannic acid treatment 2
Pre-mordant: Alum 2
Dye: 300% Weld
Over dye: 0.3g Indigo,
15-min dip x 1

193
Follow recipe 186
Over dye 2: 3g Indigo,
5-min dip x 3

194
Follow recipe 186
Over dye 2: 3g Indigo,
5-min dip x 2

195
Follow recipe 186
Over dye 2: 3g Indigo,
5-min dip x 1

196
Follow recipe 186
Over dye 2: 4g Indigo,
5-min dip x 3

197
Follow recipe 186
Over dye 2: 4g Indigo,
5-min dip x 2

198
Follow recipe 186
Over dye 2: 4g Indigo,
5-min dip x 1

RECIPES: ALL RECIPES ARE BASED ON THE BASIC TREATMENT, MORDANT AND DYE RECIPES IN PART ONE: TREATMENTS AND MORDANTS *SEE* PP.28–9, DYES *SEE* PP.37–8. ANY VARIATIONS FROM THE BASIC RECIPES, OR STEPS PARTICULAR TO THE INDIVIDUAL RECIPES, ARE WRITTEN IN *ITALICS*.

QUANTITIES: ALL QUANTITIES ARE GIVEN FOR 100G OF YARN (DRY WEIGHT).   **WATER PH:** ALL RECIPES USE WATER PH 7 (*SEE* P.21).

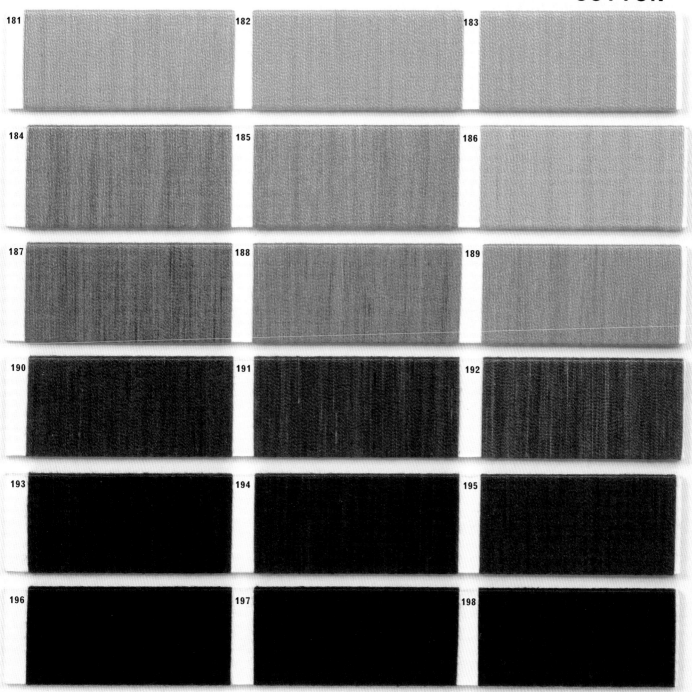

181
182
183
184
185
186
187
188
189
190
191
192
193
194
195
196
197
198

KHAKI – GREEN RECIPES FOR VEGETABLE FIBRES

Iron can darken and dull a colour if it is used as a mordant before dyeing. It can also have an effect of bleaching out the pigment if used as an after mordant. The temperature and length of time also varies the result, as does adding iron to the dye bath as opposed to making a separate mordant bath.

199
Tannic acid treatment 2
Pre-mordant: Alum 2
Dye: 200% Weld
After mordant: 0.5% Iron,
simmer for 20 min

200
Tannic acid treatment 2
Pre-mordant: Alum 2
Dye: 100% Weld
After mordant: 0.5% Iron,
simmer for 20 min

201
Tannic acid treatment 2
Pre-mordant: Alum 2
Dye: 50% Weld
After mordant: 0.5% Iron,
simmer for 20 min

202
Tannic acid treatment 2
Pre-mordant: Alum 2
Dye: Weld 1st exhaust from
recipe 205

203
Tannic acid treatment 2
Pre-mordant: Alum 2
Dye: Weld 1st exhaust from
recipe 206

204
Tannic acid treatment 2
Pre-mordant: Alum 2
Dye: Weld 1st exhaust from
recipe 207

205
Tannic acid treatment 2
Pre-mordant: Alum 2
Dye: 500% Weld
After mordant: 2% Iron,
add to dye bath for 20 min

206
Tannic acid treatment 2
Pre-mordant: Alum 2
Dye: 300% Weld
After mordant: 2% Iron,
add to dye bath for 20 min

207
Tannic acid treatment 2
Pre-mordant: Alum 2
Dye: 150% Weld
After mordant: 2% Iron,
add to dye bath for 20 min

208
Follow recipe 199
Over dye: 0.25g Indigo,
in-out dip x 1

209
Follow recipe 200
Over dye: 0.25g Indigo,
in-out dip x 1

210
Follow recipe 201
Over dye: 0.25g Indigo,
in-out dip x 1

211
Follow recipe 202
Over dye: 0.5g Indigo,
1-min dip x 4

212
Follow recipe 203
Over dye: 0.5g Indigo,
1-min dip x 2

213
Follow recipe 204
Over dye: 0.5g Indigo,
in-out dip x 1

214
Follow recipe 205
Over dye: 4g Indigo,
in-out dip x 4

215
Follow recipe 206
Over dye: 4g Indigo,
1-min dip x 2

216
Follow recipe 207
Over dye: 4g Indigo,
1-min dip x 1

RECIPES: ALL RECIPES ARE BASED ON THE BASIC TREATMENT, MORDANT AND DYE RECIPES IN PART ONE: TREATMENTS AND MORDANTS *SEE* PP.28–9, DYES *SEE* PP.37–8. ANY VARIATIONS FROM THE BASIC RECIPES, OR STEPS PARTICULAR TO THE INDIVIDUAL RECIPES, ARE WRITTEN IN *ITALICS*.

QUANTITIES: ALL QUANTITIES ARE GIVEN FOR 100G OF YARN (DRY WEIGHT). WATER PH: ALL RECIPES USE WATER PH 7 (*SEE* P.21).

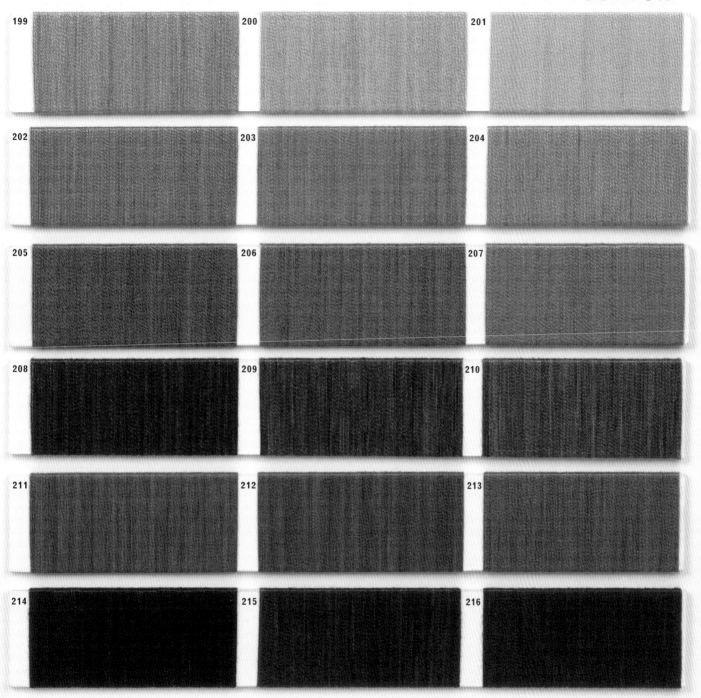

199 200 201
202 203 204
205 206 207
208 209 210
211 212 213
214 215 216

BROWN RECIPES FOR VEGETABLE FIBRES

Apart from recipes 217–19, which use just tannic acid and iron, the other colours have all been dyed with cutch. Shades 229–231 are interesting as the copper mordant seems to bring out the pink quality in the cutch. Without a mordant, the cutch looks yellower (shades 220–2), while with iron as a mordant it looks greyish pink (shades 223–5).

217
No mordant
Tannic acid treatment 2
After mordant: 2% Iron, *soak in hot-water dye bath for 10 min*

218
No mordant
Tannic acid treatment 2
After mordant: 2% Iron, *soak in warm-water dye bath for 10 min*

219
No mordant
Tannic acid treatment 2
After mordant: 2% Iron, *soak in cold-water dye bath for 10 min*

220
No mordant
Tannic acid treatment 1
Dye: 10% Cutch

221
No mordant
Tannic acid treatment 1
Dye: 5% Cutch

222
No mordant
Tannic acid treatment 1
Dye: 2.5% Cutch

223
Follow recipe 220
After mordant: 2% Iron, *simmer for 20 min*

224
Follow recipe 221
After mordant: 2% Iron, *simmer for 20 min*

225
Follow recipe 222
After mordant: 2% Iron, *simmer for 20 min*

226
Tannic acid treatment 2
Pre-mordant: Alum 2
Dye: 100% Cutch

227
Tannic acid treatment 2
Pre-mordant: Alum 2
Dye: 50% Cutch

228
Tannic acid treatment 2
Pre-mordant: Alum 2
Dye: 25% Cutch

229
Tannic acid treatment 2
Pre-mordant 1: Alum 2
Pre-mordant 2: Copper
Dye: 100% Cutch

230
Tannic acid treatment 2
Pre-mordant 1: Alum 2
Pre-mordant 2: Copper
Dye: 50% Cutch

231
Tannic acid treatment 2
Pre-mordant 1: Alum 2
Pre-mordant 2: Copper
Dye: 25% Cutch

232
No mordant
Tannic acid treatment 2
Dye: 50% Cutch
Over dye: 0.25g Indigo, *1-min dip x 2*

233
No mordant
Tannic acid treatment 2
Dye: 50% Cutch
Over dye: 0.25g Indigo, *in-out dip x 1*

234
No mordant
Tannic acid treatment 2
Dye: 50% Cutch

RECIPES: ALL RECIPES ARE BASED ON THE BASIC TREATMENT, MORDANT AND DYE RECIPES IN PART ONE: TREATMENTS AND MORDANTS *SEE* PP.28–9, DYES *SEE* PP.37–8. ANY VARIATIONS FROM THE BASIC RECIPES, OR STEPS PARTICULAR TO THE INDIVIDUAL RECIPES, ARE WRITTEN IN *ITALICS*.

QUANTITIES: ALL QUANTITIES ARE GIVEN FOR 100G OF YARN (DRY WEIGHT).   WATER PH: ALL RECIPES USE WATER PH 7 (*SEE* P.21).

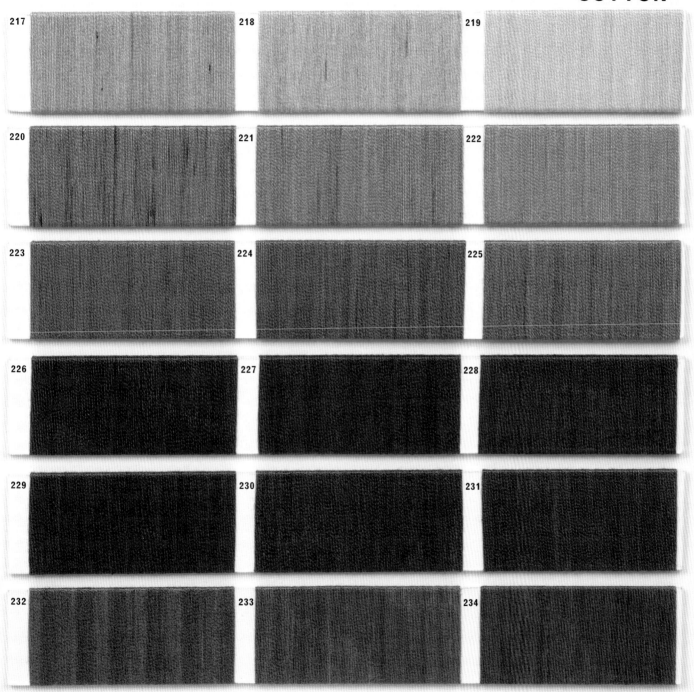

217
218
219
220
221
222
223
224
225
226
227
228
229
230
231
232
233
234

MISCELLANEOUS RECIPES FOR VEGETABLE FIBRES

It is difficult to obtain an even colour with indigo, especially with pale shades. But there are many interesting colours that can be obtained with over dyeing indigo onto previously dyed yarn. More control can be achieved with pale weak vats and multiple dips.

235
No mordant
Tannic acid treatment 2
Dye: 2.5% Cutch
Over dye: 0.25g Indigo,
1-min dip x 2

236
No mordant
Tannic acid treatment 2
Dye: 2.5% Cutch
Over dye: 0.25g Indigo,
1-min dip x 1

237
No mordant
Tannic acid treatment 2
Dye: 2.5% Cutch see p.36
Over dye: 0.25g Indigo,
in-out dip x 1

238
Follow recipe 235
Over dye: 12.5% Weld,
simmer for 20 min

239
Follow recipe 236
Over dye: 6.25% Weld,
simmer for 20 min

240
Follow recipe 237
Over dye: 3% Weld,
simmer for 20 min

241
Follow recipe 137
Over dye: 10% Cutch

242
Follow recipe 137
Over dye: *Cutch 1st exhaust
from recipe 241*

243
Follow recipe 137
Over dye: *Cutch 2nd exhaust
from recipe 241*

244
No mordant
Tannic acid treatment 2
Dye: 5% Cutch
Over dye: 0.25g Indigo,
1-min dip x 3

245
Tannic acid treatment 2
Dye: 5% Cutch
Over dye: 0.25g Indigo,
1-min dip x 1

246
Tannic acid treatment 2
Dye: 5% Cutch
Over dye: 0.25g Indigo,
in-out dip x 1

247
Tannic acid treatment 2
Pre-mordant: Alum 2
Dye: 10% Cutch
Over dye: 0.5g Indigo,
1-min dip x 4

248
Tannic acid treatment 2
Pre-mordant: Alum 2
Dye: 10% Cutch
Over dye: 0.5g Indigo,
1-min dip x 1

249
Tannic acid treatment 2
Pre-mordant: Alum 2
Dye: 10% Cutch
Over dye: 0.25g Indigo,
in-out dip x 1

250
Tannic acid treatment 2
Pre-mordant: Alum 2
Dye: 100% Cutch
Over dye: 5g Indigo,
2-min dip x 4

251
Tannic acid treatment 2
Pre-mordant: Alum 2
Dye: 100% Cutch
Over dye: 5g Indigo,
2-min dip x 1

252
Tannic acid treatment
Pre-mordant: Alum
Dye: 100% Cutch
Over dye: 1g Indigo,
in-out dip x 1

RECIPES: ALL RECIPES ARE BASED ON THE BASIC TREATMENT, MORDANT AND DYE RECIPES IN PART ONE: TREATMENTS AND MORDANTS *SEE* PP.28–9, DYES *SEE* PP.37–8. ANY VARIATIONS FROM THE BASIC RECIPES, OR STEPS PARTICULAR TO THE INDIVIDUAL RECIPES, ARE WRITTEN IN *ITALICS*.
QUANTITIES: ALL QUANTITIES ARE GIVEN FOR 100G OF YARN (DRY WEIGHT). **WATER PH:** ALL RECIPES USE WATER PH 7 (*SEE* P.21).

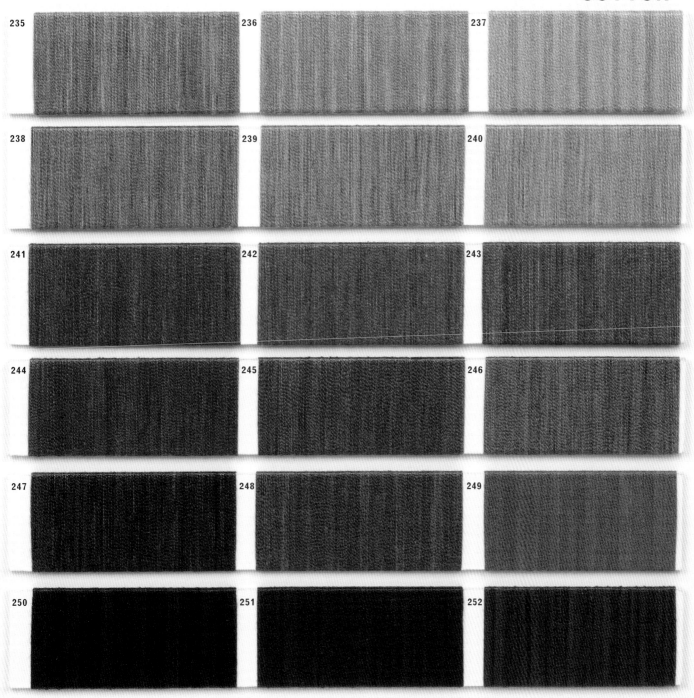

235
236
237
238
239
240
241
242
243
244
245
246
247
248
249
250
251
252

FURTHER READING

Adrosko, R.J. *Natural Dyes and Home Dyeing*, New York, Dover Publications, 1971

Albers, Josef. *Interaction of Colour*, New Haven, Yale University Press, 1975

Balfour-Paul, Jenny. *Indigo*, London, The British Museum Press, 1998

Bemis, Elijah. *The Dyer's Companion*, New York, Dover Publications, 1973 (Reprint from 1815)

Brooklyn Botanic Gardens, *Dye Plants and Dyeing*, Vol. 20, No. 3, 1964, 1972

Cannon, John and Margaret. *Dye Plants and Dyeing*, London, Herbert Press, 1994

Casselman, Karen, Leigh. *Craft of The Dyer, Colour Plants and Lichens*, New York, Dover Publications, 1993

Chandramouli, K.V., Mohanty, B.C. and Naik, H.D. *Natural Dyeing Processes of India*, Calico Museum, Ahmedabad, India, 1987

Chandramouli, K.V. *Sources of Natural Dyes in India: A Compendium with Regional Names*, Adyar, Madras, PPST Foundation, 1995

CIBA Reviews

Cumming, R. and Porter, T. *The Colour Eye*, BBC Books, 1990

Dalby, Gill. *Natural Dyes, Fast or Fugitive*, Somerset, Ashill Publications, 1985

Dalby, Gill. *Natural Dyes for Vegetable Fibres*, Somerset, Ashill Publications, 1992

Dean, Jenny. *Natural Dyeing Without Chemicals*, Bedfordshire, 1996

Dean, Jenny. *The Craft of Natural Dyeing*, Kent, Search Press, 1994

Dean, Jenny. *Wild Colour*, London, Mitchell Beazley, 1999

Delmare, Francois and Guieau, Brenard. *Colour Making and Using Dyes and Pigments*, London, Thames & Hudson, 1999

Edmonds, John. Historic Dyes Series, No.1, 1989 & No.2, 1999

Fraser, Jean. *Traditional Scottish Dyes and How to Make Them*, Edinburgh, Canongate Publishers, 1983

Gage, John. *Colour and Culture*, London, Thames & Hudson, 1993

Grierson, Su. *The Colour Cauldron*, Loveland, Interweave Press, 1988

Hummell, J.J. *The Dyeing of Textile Fabrics*, London, Cassell & Co, 1886.

Hurst, George, H. *Dyeing and Cleaning*, London, Charles Griffin & Co, 1901

Itten, Johannes. *The Elements of Colour: a Treatise on the Colour System of Johannes Itten*, New York, Chapman & Hall, 1997

Knecht, E., Rawson, G. and Lowenthal, R. *A Manual of Dyeing*, Vols. 1 & 2, London, G. Griffen & Co Ltd, 1920

Mairet, Ethel. *Vegetable Dyes*, London, Faber & Faber, 1916, 1944

Napier, James. *A Manual of Dyeing Receipts*, London, Richard Griffin & Co, 1855

Partridge, William. *A Practical Treatise on Dyeing*, Wiltshire, Pasold Research Fund, 1973 (Reprint from 1823)

Ponting, K.G. *A Dictionary of Dyes and Dyeing*, London, Bell & Hyman, 1981

Rajappa, J., Aggarwal, A., and Srivida, J. *Resource File on Natural Dyes*, Adyar Madras, PPST Foundation, 1995

Robertson, Seonaid. *Dyes From Plants*, New York, Van Nostrand Reinhold, 1973

Rutty, John, M.D. *Indigenous Vegetables Useful in Dyeing and Painting*, Dublin, 1772 (Reprint 1990, Dept. of Continuing Education, University of Bristol)

Sandberg, Gösta. *Indigo Textiles: Technique and History*, London, A & C Black, 1989

Sandberg, Gösta. *The Red Dyes: Cochineal, Madder, and Murex Purple*, NC, Lark Books, 1997

Shroff, H.B. and Trivedi, D.M. *Some Indian Indigenous Dyes and their Application*, Series No. 7, Department of Industries and Commerce UP, 1946

Simmons, Jenni. *The Shetland Dye Book*, Shetland Times, 1990

The Editors of American Fabrics and Fashion Magazine. *The New Encyclopedia of Textiles*, USA, Doric Publishing, 1960, 1972, 1980

Thurstan, Violetta. *The Use of Vegetable Dyes*, Leicester, Dryad Handicrafts, 1949

USEFUL ADDRESSES

The Association of the Guilds of Weavers, Spinners and Dyers, 3, Gatchell Meadow, Trull, Taunton, Somerset TA3 7HY

British Standards Institution, 389 Chiswick High Road, London W4 4AL

Tintometer Ltd, The Colour Laboratory, Waterloo Road, Salisbury, Wiltshire SP1 2JY

The Colour Museum Bradford, Perkin House, PO Box 244, Providence Street, Bradford, West Yorkshire BD1 2PW

The Society of Dyers and Colourists (SODC), Perkin House, 82 Gratton Road, Bradford BD1 2JB

Dyes and equipment suppliers:
Ashill Colour Studio, P. and M. Woolcraft, Pindon End, Hanslope, Milton Keynes MK19 7HN

George Weil Fibrecrafts, Old Portsmouth Road, Peasmarsh, Guildford, Surrey GU3 1LZ

The Handweavers Studio & Gallery Ltd, 29 Haroldstone Road, London E17 7AN

INDEX

Illustrations from PART ONE are written in *italics*
PART TWO is indexed according to colour

CONVERSION CHART

WEIGHTS AND MEASURES
Metric with approximate Imperial and
American equivalents:

1 gram	=	0.04 ounce
100 grams	=	3.53 ounces
5ml	=	1 teaspoon
15ml	=	1 tablespoon
30ml	=	1 fluid ounce
1 litre	=	1.76 pints
		2.13 US pints

TEMPERATURE
To convert from Centigrade to Fahrenheit:

$$9 \times {}^{\circ}C/_{5} - 32 = {}^{\circ}F$$

ACKNOWLEDGEMENTS

Author's acknowledgement
The author would like to thank Margaret Bide,
Laura Brockbank, City & Islington College, Gill Dalby,
Chris Jennings, Sara Pimpaneau, Clive Roger Oriental
Rugs, The Surrey Institute of Art & Design/University
College, Amelia Uden, Melanie Walls, Peter White and
Katarina Zahalkova.

Publisher's acknowledgement
We would like to thank Michele Clarke for the index, Chris
Jennings for the artwork, Anderley Moore for proofreading
and Amelia Uden.

First published in 2003 by The British Museum Press
A division of The British Museum Company Ltd
46 Bloomsbury Street, London WC1B 3QQ

A catalogue record for this book is available from the
British Library

ISBN 0 7141 2565 2

Commissioning Editor: Suzannah Dick
Editors: Caroline Brooke Johnson & Coralie Hepburn
Designer: Alison Fenton
Photographers: Sandra Lane & Peter White
(FXP Photography)

Reproduction by the Saxon Group, Norwich
Printing and binding in China by C&C Offset